WHEN ENOUGH IS ENOUGH

WHEN
ENOUGH IS
ENOUGH

WHEN ENOUGH IS ENOUGH

A Christian Framework for Environmental Sustainability

Edited by **R. J. Berry**

APOLLOS (an imprint of Inter-Varsity Press)
Norton Street, Nottingham NG7 3HR, England
Email: ivp@ivpbooks.com
Website: www.ivpbooks.com

Unless otherwise stated, Scripture quotations in this publication are from the Holy Bible, New International Version. Copyright © 1973, 1978, 1984 by International Bible Society. First published in Great Britain in 1979. Used by permission of Hodder & Stoughton, a division of Hodder Headline Ltd. All rights reserved. 'NIV' is a trademark of International Bible Society. UK trademark number 1448790.

Scripture quotations marked REB are taken from the Revised English Bible © Oxford University Press and Cambridge University Press 1989.

First published 2007

British Library Cataloguing in Publication Data
A catalogue record for this book is available from the British Library.

ISBN: 978-1-84474-180-9

Set in Monotype Garamond 11/13pt
Typeset in Great Britain by Servis Filmsetting Ltd, Manchester
Printed and bound in Great Britain by Ashford Colour Press Ltd, Gosport, Hampshire

Inter-Varsity Press publishes Christian books that are true to the Bible and that communicate the gospel, develop discipleship and strengthen the church for its mission in the world.

Inter-Varsity Press is closely linked with the Universities and Colleges Christian Fellowship, a student movement connecting Christian Unions in universities and colleges throughout Great Britain, and a member movement of the International Fellowship of Evangelical Students. Website: www.uccf.org.uk

CONTENTS

FOREWORD

In my book *Jesus and the Earth* I drew attention to the collection of verses in the Gospels where Jesus refers to himself as 'Son of Man', and where in the same context there is a reference to the earth. There is continuing theological debate about the meaning of this title. The reason why this collection deserves some special study is that, whatever else the phrase signifies, the 'Son of Man' in Hebrew means, 'The Son of the One from the Earth'. To find Jesus referring to himself in this way while in the same breath talking about the earth merits serious attention, not least because if you asked many Christians whether or not Jesus had anything to say about the earth, they would be hard-pressed to give a positive answer.

Further to my own studies and relevant to this book on environmental sustainability we find Jesus asking at the end of one of his parables, 'However, when the Son of Man comes, will he find faith on the earth?' (Luke 18:8).

Jesus had just told the story of the nagging widow who pesters a judge for a ruling in a dispute with an opponent. We are not told the nature of the grievance. That is irrelevant to the point of the parable, where Jesus said we 'should always pray and not give up' (Luke 18:1). The judge is eventually worn down by her bothering and grants her justice. Jesus spells out the meaning: 'And will not God bring about justice . . . I tell you, he will see that they get justice, and quickly' (vv. 7–8).

In Luke's Gospel, the purview of prayer is the coming of the kingdom of the good Father (Luke 11:1–13). Luke acknowledges that one of the issues for the disciples of Jesus (both then and now) is why after so much prayer we are still waiting, and he recognizes therefore that one of the great temptations is to lose heart and give up.

When the kingdom of God is eventually established, his reign will be marked by justice. This is a constant theme throughout the Bible. And here in this parable the judge gives the widow justice, prompting Jesus to promise that one day God too will grant justice to those 'who cry out to him day and night' (Luke 18:7).

As the pages of this book show, the root cause of an unsustainable world is the lack of justice. The three great Abrahamic faiths, Judaism, Christianity and Islam, believe that not only is God merciful but he is also just. Indeed, without justice there can be no mercy, for the latter implies the former. In Christianity, there is a remarkable claim that through Jesus the human race and the whole of creation are reconciled to God. You cannot be made one with the God of justice without at the same time being caught up in the dynamic divine passion to see his justice established on the face of the earth. That is why Jesus taught his followers to pray not only that the kingdom of God would come but also that God's will would be done *on earth* as it is in heaven. It is a prayer for the earthing of heaven, the earthing of justice.

So, the Son of Man who was of both earth and heaven and whose mission is to unify the two, urges his followers to keep on praying for the earthing of heaven 'and not give up'. Jesus assures us that God will one day grant us justice and challenges us to keep the 'faith on the earth'. God knows it is not easy to stay faithful. So much militates against a fair, free and sustainable world, as the chapters here show. But, although Christians have mostly come late to understanding what is happening to the earth (with the prophetic voice coming from beyond the walls of the church), the gospel of Jesus Christ lays upon us unavoidable responsibility to change, and at the same time calls us to have faith in and work with God, who is the sustainer of all.

The Rt Revd James Jones
Bishop of Liverpool

EDITOR'S NOTE

All the chapters in this book (with the exception of that by Joanne Green, which was written specially) are revised and updated versions of papers given at a joint Conference of Christians in Science, the John Ray Initiative and the Victoria Institute on 'The Christian Framework for Sustainability', in London, 1 October 2005.

As editor, I have attempted to remove major overlaps between chapters, but not to eliminate all repetition. For example, many of the authors quote the Brundtland Report definition of 'sustainable development' and use it to examine our responsibility to future generations. This is clearly an important element of any treatment of sustainability and it would be wrong to diminish it by overzealous editing. Nor have I tried to impose any uniformity between chapters. For example, the chapter by Donald Hay deals with concepts and debates used by professional economists; it is proper that these should be aired and criticized in their own right and not forced into a common mould with (say) the biblical approach of Dave Bookless or the scientific exposition of John Houghton. With a topic like 'sustainability', which impinges on so many facets of life and faith, it seems better to expose readers to a breadth of inputs than seek an artificial homogeneity. For similar reasons, I have included the citations given by the authors to justify their statements so that their arguments and conclusions can be followed up. This has resulted in a longer references section than is common in a book of this nature, but it seems worthwhile in the context. As environmental sustainability is a subject on the margins of most Christians' awareness, it is appropriate that they should have sources to test its data and challenges for themselves.

R. J. Berry

1. SUSTAINABILITY: GOD'S WAY OR GREENWASH?

R. J. Berry

R. J. (Sam) Berry, DSc, FRSE, was Professor of Genetics at University College London 1978–2000. He is a former President of the Linnean Society, the British Ecological Society, the European Ecological Federation, the Mammal Society and Christians in Science. He received the Templeton UK Award in 1996 for his 'sustained advocacy of the Christian faith in the world of science'. Sam Berry is the author of God and Evolution *(Hodder & Stoughton, 1988, 2001),* God and the Biologist *(Apollos, 1996) and* God's Book of Works *(Continuum, 2003), and editor of* Environmental Dilemmas *(Chapman & Hall, 1993),* The Care of Creation *(IVP, 2000) and* Environmental Stewardship *(Continuum, 2006). He chairs the Environmental Issues Network of Churches Together in Britain and Ireland and is Vice-President of the John Ray Initiative.*

In 1975, John Taylor, newly moved from being General Secretary of the Church Missionary Society to being Bishop of Winchester, wrote a widely read little book, *Enough Is Enough*. His prompt was the concern elicited by the publication of *A Blueprint for Survival* (*The Ecologist* 1972), a manifesto for restraint and reordering of our demands upon the environment drawn up by the editorial team of

a recently founded (1971) journal, *The Ecologist*. The *Blueprint* itself
was based on a computer simulation at the Massachusetts Institute
of Technology, which showed how population growth, agricultural practices, resource-use, industry and pollution interacted with
each other, resulting in inevitable 'limits to growth' with potential
effects on our quality of life (Meadows et al. 1972; see pp. 100, 111
below). Many leading UK biologists formally endorsed the
Blueprint;[1] the first leader in *The Times* on the day it was published
was headed 'The prophets may be right'.

    (The year 1972 was a key one in the development of environmen-
tal awareness.) Besides the publication of the *Blueprint* and the
Limits to Growth report, the first major international conference
devoted to the environment, the UN Conference on the Human
Environment, took place in Stockholm. I wrote a small book at the
request of IVP to help Christians relate to this growing interest
(Berry 1972). There seemed little Christian thinking to base it on.
In retrospect, a Chicago Lutheran theologian, Joseph Sittler, should
be recognized as a pioneer on the basis of a significant article that
came out in 1954, but he wrote opaquely and his work was largely
forgotten (Bouma-Prediger & Bakken 2000). At the end of the
1960s, a Church of England Report, *Man in His Living Environment*,
prepared as a contribution to the Stockholm Conference, appeared
(1969); and also in 1969, Hugh Montefiore raised questions about
the sustainability of our way of life in *The Question Mark*.

    These were the first substantial contributions to Christian envir-
onmental thought in Britain. They arose not from natural
theological enquiry, but from a secular unease stimulated by
Rachel Carson's *Silent Spring* (1962) and the saga of the oil tanker
Torrey Canyon, wrecked off Land's End in 1967, which leaked oil on

---

1. Thirty-three names were attached to the document itself, including such
   well-known scientists as Fraser Darling, Julian Huxley, David Lack,
   Aubrey Manning, Peter Scott; a further fifty signed a letter to *The Times* (25
   January 1972), welcoming 'the document as a major contribution to
   current debate . . . There is now no escape from the necessity of a
   fundamental rethinking of all our working assumptions about human
   development in relation to the world we live in.'

to many of the holiday beaches of Devon and Cornwall. Francis Schaeffer published his *Pollution and the Death of Man* in 1970, which drew the attention of his readers to Lynn White's (1967) indictment of Christian attitudes to the natural world, but did not much advance our general understanding. Finally, John Cobb's *Is It Too Late?* appeared in 1972, beginning a stream of theological writing on the environment that has concentrated on process thought and panentheism; this has been particularly influential among North American liberal theologians.

The problems of the 1970s are still with us, intensified by the growing evidence of climate change (Chapter 3), agricultural dilemmas (Chapter 7), water demands (Chapter 8) and waste mountains (Chapter 9). In his book, John Taylor suggested that a way forward might be some form of community living, perhaps on the pattern of Israeli kibbutzim. This proposal did not attract more than a minority enthusiasm, and it has been overtaken by many other ideas since the 1970s. Some of the background to this thinking is described in the following chapters. This is emphatically not a 'how to' manual; rather, it is an introduction and survey of Christian thinking about our responsibilities in this life and the future of both ourselves and our children. And, as in all areas of life, we need to work out our own responses to such understanding.

The Lord is coming – soon

I once belonged to a church that had never owned a house for its vicar. The story was that when the parish was established in 1860, the expectation was that the Lord would come again very soon and it was far more important that church members should concentrate on preaching the gospel in every land than worry about anything here on Earth. This was patently faithful to Scripture. Jesus told us, 'Do not be anxious about tomorrow; tomorrow will look after itself' (Matt. 6:34).[2] He repeatedly warned his followers

---

2. All Scripture quotations in this chapter are from the Revised English Bible.

to be prepared for the coming of 'the kingdom'. His last words on earth were, 'Go to all nations' (Matt. 28:19). And Peter wrote that 'the heavens will disappear with a great rushing sound, the elements will be dissolved in flames, and the earth and all that is in it will be brought to judgement' (2 Pet. 3:10).

The Bible's teaching seems incontrovertible: forget this world: the more faithful you are in proclaiming Christ's saving work at all times and in all places, the sooner Christ will come again in glory and take us all to be with him in heaven. Ronald Reagan's Secretary for the Interior, James Watt, testified to a Senate Committee that he believed the return of Christ was imminent, a belief that influenced his and Reagan's agenda (and that of the subsequent Bush administrations) under which many environmental regulations were torn up (Northcott 2004: 67; see also Bratton 1983). Watt was manifesting a premillennialist or dispensationalist position, once favoured by evangelicals (not least because of the popularity of the 'Scofield Bible Notes'). Michael Northcott (2004: 59) has commented, 'The premillennialist scorns all efforts to correct the ills of society for to inaugurate any programme of social betterment would be to thwart the divine purpose and to delay the advent of Christ.' Such an interpretation remains common in North America, but has largely been replaced in Europe by amillennialism or postmillennialism, mainly as a result of looking afresh at the Scriptures (Finger 1998). When our Lord spoke about not being anxious about tomorrow, his message was God's overriding and controlling providence. In the same passage, he says God feeds the birds and 'clothes the grass' (Matt. 6:26, 30). Just before Peter writes about the heavens disappearing and the elements melting, he tells us 'the first world was destroyed by water, the water of the flood' (2 Pet. 3:6). Now it is apparent that the first world was not *destroyed* by Noah's flood, or we would not be here now; what happened is that God purged the earth through the flood, and it is reasonable to assume that he will use fire to purge our current world, just as Paul says he will (1 Cor. 3:13). Moreover, we will not 'go up' to heaven; the new Jerusalem will come down *from* heaven, so that the dwelling of God will be with his creatures:

> Eventually heaven and earth will not be separated, but in being renewed, will be integrated with each other. The great claim of Revelation 21 and

22 is that heaven and earth will finally be united. This is the polar
opposite of all kinds of Gnosticism with their ultimate separation of
heaven and earth – a worldview that is all too suspiciously close to some
forms of devout Western Christianity. (Wright 1999a: 10)

This is not the place to enter into the debates about the coming
judgment and conflicting interpretations about the Millennium,
Armageddon and the Apocalypse; they inflame passions and
consume lives (sometimes literally) (Boyer 1992; Sizer 2004). The
need here is to examine the biblical passages used in such debates
and learn from them (and the rest of the Scriptures) what God
wants from us in our present existence. And there can be little
doubt that he has given us the job as his agents of caring for and
nurturing this world (Gen. 2:15; Ps. 115:16) and that we will be
held accountable to him for our treatment of that which he has
entrusted to us (Matt. 25:14–30). For his part, God made an 'everlasting covenant' to maintain 'all living creatures' (Gen. 9:8–17),
long before the covenant he made with Abraham and his descendants (Gen. 17:9). He led his covenant people into a 'good land . . .
where you will never suffer any scarcity of food to eat, nor want
for anything' (Deut. 8:7–10). We must beware any interpretation
that separates the two covenants; Christ's death on the cross 'reconciled *all things* to him [God] – *all things*, whether on earth or in
heaven' (Col. 1:20). In other words, salvation extends beyond
humankind to all creation.

As evangelicals, we pride ourselves on being men and women of
the Bible. If we are consistent in this profession, we have to see
beyond a proper zeal for evangelism and the second coming to a
God-given care for creation. What does this mean in practice?

Historical context

For almost all human history, we have assumed that the world's
resources are effectively inexhaustible. In theological terms, the
belief has been that God provides lavishly and unstintingly for
humankind, singling us out because he loves us as those alone
made in his image. There have been repeated reasons to doubt

this divine provision: China alone has had around two thousand famines in the last two thousand years; overpopulation and land scarcity have led to successive mass emigrations – the Beaker Folk, Teutons, Vikings and New World colonizers have all spilled from the western seaboard of Europe. Mismanagement has often produced disastrous consequences: the early Polynesian population of New Zealand depended on the large flightless Moas for food, but managed to drive them to extinction within six hundred years; overextension of irrigation was a major factor in the collapse of the ancient Babylonian Empire; Sicily was once the granary of Italy but less and less grain is grown there as the soil deteriorates under excessive cultivation and goat browsing; the ecological implosion of Easter Island is well documented.

In retrospect, presuming on the infallible fruitfulness of 'nature' has led to the almost inevitable collapse of a wide range of different societies. Frightening examples of these have been persuasively chronicled by Jared Diamond (2005), who identifies five underlying and interacting causes:

1. Environmental damage.
2. Climate change.
3. Hostile neighbours.
4. Trade partners.
5. Response to symptoms of stress.

Diamond documents how the first four of these vary in importance in different situations, but the fifth is always significant.

Actually, the assumption that God will always provide without limit is unfounded: the Bible is explicit that his bounty is conditional on our obedience, beginning with Eden (we are commanded to 'look after' the garden: Gen. 2:17), through various testings of ancient Israel (Deut. 6:23–25), to our life as the redeemed in Christ (Heb. 5:9; 1 Pet. 1:22; 1 John 2:3; Rev. 12:17). As we have noted, this obedience involves caring for creation, a relationship usually described as 'stewardship' (Granberg-Michaelson 1987; Brandt 2002). Although aspects of stewardship have been criticized (Palmer 1992; Gould 1993; Lovelock 1995; Hore-Lacy 2006; and see Chapter 2, pp. 44–45) and glossed over (e.g. Santmire 2003), the notion that we are responsible for our use of the earth's resources is robust and remains strong, whether we call it 'stewardship', 'trusteeship', 'co-creatorship', 'guardianing' or simply 'creation care' (Hall 1986; Berry 2006). The Old Testament in particular is full of examples and warnings about environmental mismanagement through poor stewardship, from either failure or neglect (e.g. Lev. 18:25, 28; 25:2–6; Deut. 29:22–25; Isa. 24:4–6; Jer. 12:10–11).

Perhaps our assumption of infinite divine provision arises from failing to distinguish between the gracious providence of God (he cares even for the birds and flowers, and the winds and waves obey him: Matt. 6:25–34; 8:27) and his explicit expectations of us (Gen. 1:28). In his comment on Genesis 2:15, Calvin (1847: 125) wrote that 'the custody of the garden was given in charge to Adam to show that we possess the things that God has committed to our hands, on the condition that being content with a frugal and moderate use of them, we should take care of what shall remain'. He goes on to speak of what we have come to call 'sustainability':

> Let him who possesses a field so partake of its yearly fruits that he may not suffer the ground to be injured by his negligence; but let him endeavour to hand it down to posterity as he received it, or even better cultivated . . . Let every one regard himself as the steward of God in all things he possesses. Then he will neither conduct himself dissolutely nor corrupt by abuse those things which God requires to be preserved. (125)

Walter Brueggemann makes a very similar point. He points out that for the author of Deuteronomy, the Promised Land in which the Israelites will lack nothing (Deut. 8:7–10) is not about the existence or prosperity of its inhabitants, but is an indissoluble partnership with both land and Yahweh, 'never only with Yahweh as to live only in intense obedience, never only with land as though simply to possess and manage' (Brueggemann 1977: 52). This produces a lasting tension for Israel – which is also a dynamic: how to hold together the Mosaic tradition that stresses obedience to Yahweh in ways that minimize the importance of the land, with the Davidic tradition that stresses the land and neglects the Torah.

A lack of Christian concern for the environment has grown with the secularization of society. Land has increasingly become a resource or commodity, rather than a gift or trust. This reduces its moral claim on us and often leads to injustice. In Britain, there were attempts to deal with this from the eighteenth century onwards by regulating the enclosure of common land. These culminated in a General Inclosure Act in 1845, which laid down that the health, comfort and convenience of local people had to be taken into account before any enclosure was sanctioned.

Over the next century this produced increasing control of land use and planning, and requirements to maintain both the use and aesthetics of the countryside. The concerns were secular, but sprang from an unspoken notion that the 'land' was creation, given to us in trust (Black 1970). Religion was not explicit, but even today often underlies the assumptions of responsible administration. The Nature Conservancy Council, a UK statutory organization, stated in 1984 that the rationale for nature conservation in Britain is 'primarily cultural, that is the conservation of wild flora and fauna, geological and physiographic features for their scientific, recreational, aesthetic and inspirational value'. 'Cultural' was defined 'as referring to the whole mental life of a nation. This cultural purpose shades imperceptibly into that which is clearly economic, that is dealing with aspects of resource utilization providing for material existence and regulated by commercial factors' (Nature Conservancy Council 1984: 75).

Notwithstanding, creation care increasingly proceeds with no acknowledgment to the Creator. Environmental concerns are almost always utilitarian, driven negatively by fear rather than positively by respect. In 1962, Rachel Carson's *Silent Spring* was a major wake-up call to ignoring natural processes gratuitously. The Limits to Growth study apparently showed that the economic and industrial systems of the developed countries would collapse about the year 2100 unless two conditions changed: birth rate should equal death rate, and capital investment should equal capital depreciation (Meadows et al. 1972). The study was disliked by economists and heavily criticized on the grounds that it ignored market forces and technological developments (Chapter 6, p. 111). Notwithstanding, it resonated widely in drawing attention to the fact that a finite system has inevitable limits, even if there is no agreement about what these are or when they will be reached. Follow-up analyses, using better data and a refined program, twenty and then thirty years after the original report merely confirmed the initial conclusions.

How should we react? In the 1960s, the debate was between proponents of 'zero population growth' and those who saw salvation coming from better and more efficiently used resources. The Limits study drew attention to the danger of ignoring human impacts: our survival depends ultimately on our rate of use of resources and whether these resources are renewable or not. It was published at the same time as the report of the UN Stockholm Conference on the Human Environment. The Stockholm Conference is generally credited with introducing into general discourse the concept of sustainability. It declared, 'A point has been reached in history when we must shape our actions throughout the world with a more prudent care for their environmental consequences. Through ignorance or indifference we can do massive and irreversible harm to the earthly environment on which our life and well-being depend' (Item 6 in the Preamble to the Declaration of the UN Conference on the Human Environment, Stockholm, 5–16 June 1972; reprinted in Birnie & Boyle 1995: 3). A basic concept was 'development without destruction' (Ward & Dubos 1972).

The Stockholm Conference stimulated a tremendous amount of concern and support for the developing world, but also a division between 'development' and 'environmental care and protection'. Looking after the environment was regarded as a much lower priority than development and attacking poverty; indeed, it was commonly regarded as a hindrance to development. In 1980, a World Conservation Strategy (WCS) was produced to counter these assumptions; it argued that development was only sustainable if it was joined to care for the environment. The WCS had three explicit aims, to

- maintain essential ecological processes and life-support systems;
- preserve genetic diversity; and, significantly,
- ensure the *sustainable* utilization of species and ecosystems.

The Strategy focused firmly on people.

Humanity's relationship with the biosphere (the thin covering of the planet that contains and sustains life) will continue to deteriorate until a new international economic order is achieved, a new environmental ethic adopted, human populations stabilize, and sustainable modes of development become the rule rather than the exception.

The implications of this were taken up by the World Commission on Environment and Development chaired by Gro Harlem Brundtland, whose report, *Our Common Future* (1987, commonly referred to as the Brundtland Report), emphasized the need to recognize ecological as well as economic interdependence among nations. The Report is remembered particularly for its definition of sustainable development: 'Development that meets the needs of the present without compromising the ability of future generations to meet their own needs' (43). Although often quoted, this definition has been heavily criticized as ambiguous and open to contradictory interpretations (Chapter 2, p. 36). Also, it ignored the 'limits to growth' constraint, implying that 'nature' can meet all human needs if social and technological deficiencies are sorted out. This belief still persists in some places: the declared policy of the US Administration under G. W. Bush, for example, states, 'Our policies should encourage innovation and the development of new, cleaner technologies'; nothing is said about responsible care or the implications of the policy for less privileged nations (for a criticism, see Rolston 2002).

The revised WCS (*Caring for the Earth* 1991), which set the scene for the United Nations Conference on the Earth and the Environment at Rio de Janeiro (the 'Earth Summit'), redefined 'sustainable development' as 'improving the quality of human life while living within the carrying capacity of supporting ecosystems' (10). It pointed out the confusion around the use of 'sustainable' as an adjective:

'Sustainable development', 'sustainable growth', and 'sustainable use' have been used interchangeably as if their meanings were the same. They are not. 'Sustainable growth' is a contradiction in terms: nothing physical can grow indefinitely. 'Sustainable use' is applicable only to renewable resources: it means using them at rates within their capacity for renewal . . . A 'sustainable economy' is the product of sustainable development. It maintains its natural resource base. It can continue to develop by adapting, and through improvements in knowledge, organization, technical efficiency and wisdom. (10)

Importantly, in the context of this book, *Caring for the Earth* called for 'a world ethic for living sustainably'. A significant criticism of the original Strategy had been that it fell into an Enlightenment fallacy by failing to emphasize that responsible behaviour towards the environment was not an inevitable result of recognizing environmental facts (Jacobs & Munro 1987).[3] *Caring for the Earth* spelt out the ethic missing from the *Word Conservation Strategy*; it included an aim that everyone should

> share fairly the benefits and costs of resource use, among different communities and interest groups, among regions that are poor and those that are affluent, and between present and future generations. Each generation should leave to the future a world that is at least as diverse and productive as the one it inherited. Development of one society or generation should not limit the opportunities of other societies or generations. (1991: 14)

In his 1990 Report, the Secretary General of the United Nations called for a Covenant on Environment and Development: 'The Charter of the United Nations governs relations between States. The Universal Declaration of Human Rights pertains to relationships between the State and the individual. The time has come to devise a covenant regulating relations between humankind and nature.' The International Environmental Law Commission responded with an 'International Covenant on Environment and

---

3. The failure of policy-makers and politicians to respond to factual information has been extensively explored by social scientists in recent years, and labelled the 'knowledge deficit' (e.g. Brunk 2006). John Lawton, Chairman of the Royal Commission on Environmental Pollution, has examined the effect of this and other factors on the reasons why scientific information is often ignored (Lawton, in the press).

Development', which codified into proposed 'hard law' the large amount of 'soft law' on the environment contained in a range of agreements and treaties, such as the Stockholm Conference, the World Charter for Nature, the Law of the Sea, and the Rio Declaration of the 'Earth Summit' of 1992. The draft Covenant has been through various revisions, most recently in 2004. It still awaits formal adoption by the international community. Notwithstanding, it represents the beginning of a convergence between the limited concerns of humankind and the wider concerns of the natural world (Berry 1999).

Two masters?

The 'world' is pressing ahead with environmental care at all levels, from the individual to the international. As Christians we are called to care for creation. Where do we meet the 'world'? Can – or should – we go along with the world's agenda?

The first thing to note is that the first word given to our first parents was to 'have dominion' over the rest of creation. Several authors in this volume note that Lynn White (1967) argued that this has been commonly interpreted as justifying unrestrained human plunder of the natural world. But as many commentators have pointed out, such an interpretation is wrong: although the word translated 'dominion' implies 'rule', the Hebrew model of kingship was of a servant (Ps. 72), not an oriental despot; moreover, the command was given in the context of humanity 'made in God's image', which implies a reciprocal relationship (e.g. Sheldon 1989; Whitney 1993). The debates and misinterpretations about White's thesis do not concern us here, although it is worth mentioning the 'confession' of a distinguished American historian, Max Oeschlaeger (1994: 1–2):

> For most of my adult life I believed, as many environmentalists do, that
> religion was the primary cause of ecological crisis (which grew out of
> my reading of Lynn White's famous essay blaming Judeo-Christianity for
> the environmental crisis). I also assumed that various experts had
> solutions to environmental malaise: if only people would listen to the

ecologists, economists, and others who made claims that they could 'manage planet Earth', we would be saved. I lost that faith by bits and pieces, especially through the demystification of two ecological problems – climate heating and the extinction of species – and by discovering the roots of my prejudice against religion.

He argues that the way forward is to accept that 'religion and science can be collaborative rather than antagonistic forms of discourse' (36).

Oeschlaeger is only one among many who emphasize the important reality that we are *all* called and mandated to care for creation, whether or not we use religious language. At the most basic level, we depend on creation for our survival. Unless we have oxygen, water and food we are doomed. The massive Millennium Ecosystem Assessment report (MA 2005; see also Chapter 5, p. 91) identified the essential constituents of human well-being as access to the basic materials for a good life (such as food, shelter and clothing), sound health, good social relations, security, freedom of choice and action. It focused on four categories of 'ecosystem services':

• *provisioning services*, such as food, water, timber, fibre;
• *regulating services*, affecting climate, flood control, disease, waste and water quality;
• *cultural services*, providing recreation, aesthetic and spiritual benefits;
• *supporting services*, such as soil formation, photosynthesis and nutrient cycling.

Jonathon Porritt (2005) has distinguished between primary ecological sustainability (which is fundamental, because without it life cannot survive) and secondary goals (such as the elimination of poverty or the attainment of universal human rights), which are subsidiary (and desirable), because they depend on learning to live within the Earth's systems and limits. He defines sustainability as the capacity for continuance into the long-term future, and sustainable development as the process by which we move towards sustainability (2005: 21).

Governments tend to concentrate on measures of economic activity and take the components of sustainability for granted (Arrow et al. 2004). British Prime Minister Tony Blair (1999: 3) has acknowledged the danger of this:

> Focusing solely on economic growth risks ignoring the impact – both good and bad – on people and on the environment . . . Governments have seemed to forget this. Success has been measured by economic growth – GDP – alone. We have failed to see how our economy, our environment and our society are all one. And that delivering the best possible quality of life for us all means more than concentrating solely on economic growth.

Ten years earlier, another British government had been even more outspoken:

> The ethical imperative of stewardship must underlie all environmental policies. Mankind has always been capable of great good and great evil. That is certainly true of our role as custodians of our planet . . . It was the Prime Minister [Margaret Thatcher] who reminded us that we do not hold a freehold on our world, but only a full repairing lease. We have a moral duty to look after our planet and to hand it on in good order to future generations. (*This Common Inheritance* 1990: 10)

The acceptance of environmental damage and the urgency to deal with it remain contentious. A well-publicized denial is that of Danish statistician Bjørn Lomborg, in a book *The Skeptical Environmentalist*, published in English in 2001. Lomborg argued that most examples of a deteriorating environment are environmentalists' hype and that our environment is actually improving. His thesis has been heavily criticized; the reviewers in *Nature* called the book 'like a compilation of term papers from one of those classes from hell where one has to fail all the students. It is a mass of poorly digested material, deeply flawed in its selection of examples and analysis' (Pimm & Harvey 2001). The journal *Scientific American* published a detailed rebuttal of its claims, concluding that Lomborg's 'seemingly dispassionate outsider's view is often marred by an incomplete use of the data or a misunderstanding of the underlying science' (2002). Lomborg himself was referred to the

Danish Committees on Scientific Dishonesty, who ruled in 2003 that 'Objectively speaking the publication of the work under consideration is deemed to fall within the concept of scientific dishonesty' (Danish Committees on Scientific Dishonesty 2003) and that Lomborg was guilty of systematic bias in his choice of data and argument (this judgment was subsequently rejected by the Danish Ministry of Science on the grounds that Lomborg's book was not established as a scientific publication).

In contrast *The Economist* (6 September 2001) described *The Skeptical Environmentalist* as 'one of the most valuable books on public policy in the last ten years' and co-sponsored a conference with Lomborg in 2004 to identify the ten greatest problems facing humanity. This conference produced a 'Copenhagen Consensus', that the prevention and treatment of HIV/AIDS was the top global priority, while the Kyoto protocol and two proposals for tax on carbon dioxide were 'bad investments' on the ground that the cost of dealing with climate change outweighed the benefits. The analyses carried out by the participants have been heavily criticized, with even *The Economist* concluding that the results 'gave rise to suspicion in some quarters that the whole exercise had been rigged'. Writing as professional economists, Felix FitzRoy and Ian Smith (2004: 707) have detailed

> how Lomborg selects statistics to support his optimistic views and systematically neglects relevant but unfavourable evidence; he ignores much of modern environmental economics, such as the use of genuine investment that captures environmental degradation, 'double dividends' from green taxation in the presence of unemployment, and local health benefits from abatement of emissions.

Lomborg is just one of a few but vociferous individuals who argue that the environment is in good health. UK Government Chief Scientist David King (2005) has commented that

> there is a small group of scientists who appear at every meeting on climate change but are not seriously regarded. These include a Danish scientist who argues, without any proper evidence, that sea levels are not rising at all; a French scientist who claims from a study of records of tea

plantation companies in Tanzania that there has been no temperature increase around Kilimanjaro despite the loss of 85% of its ice cap (which has been dated back to the last ice age) over the past 100 years; and a British scientist who says that global warming is happening but is due to increased solar activity.

In the USA, Calvin Beisner (1997) has been a long-standing opponent of environmentalism,[4] most recently taking the lead in attacking American evangelicals concerned about global warming (Spencer, Driessen & Beisner 2005). Beisner's arguments are based on an extremely high view of human potential, to the extent of seeking ways to reverse the effects of the curse of Genesis 3 by a renewed commitment to the dominion and stewardship mandates of Genesis 1:28 and 2:15.[5]

---

4. Leal (2005: 366) describes Beisner's book *Where Garden Meets Wilderness* as 'aggressively conservative, both theologically and politically, and at times reads more like a defence of the political and economic status quo in North America rather than a specifically theological study'.

5. It is an idea cruelly parodied by Donald Worster (1993: 9), an American historian: 'The key American environmental idea, and at once the most destructive and most creative, the most complacent and most radical, is the one that ironically has about it an aura of wonderful innocence. America, we have believed, is literally the Garden of Eden restored . . . Adam and Eve, discovering evil after yielding to the Devil's temptation, had to be kicked out of the Garden on their nearly naked bums. But *mirabile dictu*, Americans of the eighteenth century found a way to sneak back into the garden. A band of their ancestors made their way to the New World and there rediscovered it, with the gate standing wide open, undefended. What a blessed people. They brought along some Africans in chains to help enjoy the place, and by and by they let in a few others from Asia, but mainly it was a fortunate band of white Europeans that destiny allowed to re-enter and repossess the long-lost paradise.' Sadly, there is more than a grain of truth in this attitude. It represents an excessive and antinomian libertarianism roundly condemned by Paul in Rom. 3:5–12. Michael Northcott (2004: 81) cites the Nobel laureate economist Friedrich Hayek as taking the same position: 'State action to improve the

Two books

As in so many areas where religion and the secular world meet, we are given an impression and legacy of conflict. Religion (particularly Judaism and Christianity) is commonly blamed for encouraging environmental misuse; many Christians regard environmental care as much less important than evangelism or poverty relief. We are mere transients and it does not matter how we treat this world.

Does the Bible give any help? An obvious starting point is Genesis 3. This describes the environmental consequences of disobeying God's commands. There are only implicit references to the events described in the chapter elsewhere in the Old Testament (Bimson 2006). Romans 8:19–22 is the New Testament passage that most clearly refers to it, as well as looking forward to what God intends to do with the cosmos. It is a difficult passage.[6] It is near the end of Paul's argument in Romans 5–8 that the renewal of God's covenant results in the renewal of God's creation (he argues similarly in 2 Cor. 3–5). The fall of Adam is expounded in Romans 1:18–32 and more explicitly in 5:12–21. Then Paul speaks of the reversal of the fall – not through human endeavour but through Christ, using explicit 'new covenant' language (Wright 1999b). When Paul writes that 'The universe itself is

---

human condition, whether to help an individual in poverty or to prevent a company from harming the environment, is invariably coercive, restrictive of individual freedom, and therefore immoral.'

6. Wright (1999a: 11) comments, 'This passage is regularly marginalized by mainstream Protestant interpretations of Romans. If you insist on reading Romans simply as a book about how human beings "get saved" in the sense of "going to heaven when they die", you will find that these verses function as a kind of odd apologetic appendix. That, in consequence, is how the tradition has often regarded them, both in the "radical" scholarship of Lutherans like Bultmann and Käsemann and in the "conservative" readings of much evangelical scholarship. In fact the passage is the deliberate climax to the whole train of thought in Romans 5–8, and indeed Romans 1–8 as a whole.'

to be freed from the shackles of mortality and is to enter upon the glorious liberty of the children of God' (v. 21), he is

> completing an analogy with the exodus from Egypt and entry into the Promised Land that he has been developing in the preceding chapters. When God's people come through the waters of baptism (paralleling the passage through the Red Sea) and so are freed from sin (slavery, in parallel with Egypt), they are given, not the Torah this time as in Sinai, but the Spirit. And it is the Spirit that will lead them into their promised land, the renewed and liberated cosmos. (Wright 1999a: 12)

Paul's message is one of hope, just as the liberation of God's people from exile is inextricably linked by Isaiah with the rejoicing of all creation (Isa. 55:12–13). Moule (1964: 12) interprets Romans 8:19–22 as meaning that

> man is responsible before God for nature. As long as man refuses to play the part assigned him by God, so long the entire world of nature is frustrated and dislocated. It is only when man is truly fitting into his proper position as a son in relation to God his father that the dislocation of nature will be reduced.

Kidner (1967: 73) argues similarly in his Tyndale Commentary on Genesis, 'Leaderless the choir of creation can only grind in discord.' Blocher (1984: 184) makes essentially the same point: 'If man obeys God, he would be the means of blessing the earth; but in his insatiable greed . . . And in his short-sighted selfishness, he pollutes and destroys it. He turns the garden into a desert (cf. Rev. 11: 18). That is the main thrust of the curse of Genesis 3.'

This reading of Scripture is important, because it focuses on the extraordinary patience and providence (and sovereignty) of God (cf. e.g. God's initiative in reconciling *all things* to himself, Col. 1:13–20) and contrasts radically with ideas that the future of the world is built upon a sophisticated version of deism (Barclay 2006). The latter supposition (which is really no more than specu-lation) is that creation matures as some sort of intrinsic unfolding. It is a concept that has repeatedly surfaced since the early twentieth century or so in philosophical speculation: in the *élan vital* of Henri Bergson, the noogenesis of Teilhard de Chardin, the panentheism of Hartshorne, Cobb and Peacocke, Lovelock's Gaia, the 'promise of nature' as advocated by John Haught (2005) and 'strong emergence' as proposed by Philip Clayton (2004). It is pertinent to recall Aubrey Moore's welcome of the banishment of deism through Darwinism, which for him 'under the disguise of a foe, did the work of a friend'. His argument was that early nineteenth-century deism had left

> God 'throned in magnificent splendour in a remote corner of the universe' and a machinery of 'secondary causes' had taken his place . . . Science had pushed the deist's God farther and farther away [until] at the moment when it seemed as if he would be thrust out altogether, Darwinism appeared and . . . conferred upon philosophy and religion an inestimable benefit by showing that we must choose between two alternatives. Either God is everywhere present in nature or He is nowhere. (Moore 1889: 99–100)

The most robust model for God's action in the world is complementarity, although exploring this is beyond the scope of this chapter (MacKay 1991; Jeeves & Berry 1998; Berry 2003).

In general and particularly relevant from the present point of view, a rewarding approach seems to be to follow the long-standing tradition that God wrote two books: a Book of Words (the Bible) and a Book of Works (creation). The books have the same author but are written in very different languages and consequently have to be understood through entirely different techniques. Reading the 'Book of Works' will always be more challenging than reading the 'Book of Words', because the latter is written in a language more familiar to us. Notwithstanding, any contradiction between the two must be false. On the title page of the *Origin of Species*, Darwin (1859) quoted from Francis Bacon, 'Let no man think or maintain that he can search too far or be too well studied in the book of God's words or in the book of God's works; but rather let men endeavour an endless proficiency in both.' Presumably, it was a discipline Darwin endorsed.

Sustaining diversity

There are many practical manuals about techniques for sustaining diversity, ranging from individual commitments to global possibilities (e.g. Carew-Reid et al. 1994; Holdgate 1996; Valerio 2004). They give the lie to the notion that environmentalism spells renunciation and withdrawal from the modern world. That was the implication of John Taylor's *Enough Is Enough* (1975), but perceptions have changed radically. As Heap and Comim (Chapter 5, p. 81 direct to our attention, the economist and Noble laureate Amartya Sen has called us to re-examine our humanness and recognize that we are more than merely consumers. He points out that we have values as well as needs, and that we cherish our ability to reason, act and participate; in an almost forgotten distinction, we are 'reasonable agents' as well as 'needy patients'. If the core meaning of sustainability involves acting 'without compromising the ability of future generations', we must preserve – and even expand – our existing freedoms (Sen 2004). Sen argues that a practice of 'sustainable consumption and production' need not lead to any sacrifice in living standards (Sen 2003: 14). His prompt that we are more than survival machines has strong religious implications. For the Christian, it reminds us that we are *Homo divinus*, creatures made in God's image, with all the characteristics and possibilities of that state, and not simply a (very) high ape (Stott 1972: 63; Berry, in the press).

As Heap and Comim also point out (p. 83), the combination of population growth and economic development is producing a class of new consumers in countries like China, India, Brazil, Mexico and Russia. Oil, fresh water and cultivatable land are going to become ever scarcer and presumably more expensive (Pimm 2001; see Chapters 4 and 8). Our present ways of living will certainly be challenged; the general assumption is that we will be unlikely to continue a sustainable lifestyle without external pressure.

Robert Costanza (2006) emphasizes that all this has enormous implications – we have treated economic growth as an end in itself, whereas it is really a means to an end. Notwithstanding, he believes there is a growing awareness that a present and future for all humanity is possible, but that it is one which must be both sustainable and desirable. He believes it is not enough for a system to be

- merely sustainable; an atrocious system could be sustainable indefinitely;
- merely desirable; desirability now may lead to misery later;
- desirable in some of its aspects but terrible in others (e.g. economic development that causes environmental and social destruction that outweighs its gains is not true development);
- sustainable and desirable for a small elite while leaving most people in sustainable misery.

The way forward is to internalize all the externalities in our calculations – to include conventional goods and services alongside contributions from nature, family, friends and other social relationships, and from health, education and fulfilling employment. The human-welfare-producing system depends on five different sorts of capital: financial, human, built, social and natural (Porritt 2005). We depend on all five; nature is not merely an optional or luxury good. In 1991, the Ecological Society of America launched a 'Sustainable Biosphere Initiative' recognizing that there are few places on earth uninfluenced by humankind (Lubchenco et al. 1992); this has matured into a sophisticated research programme focused on the problems of dealing with increasing demands on a finite world (Palmer et al. 2004).

An important implication of the interdependence of these different sorts of capital is that the focus of sustainability has to change: sustainable consumption will have to replace sustainable development (Chapter 5). There are signs that such a shift may be possible. More and more studies are showing that higher income and material prosperity do not simply translate into greater happiness (Myers 1992; Kasser 2002; Donovan & Halpern 2002; Schoch 2006). Jackson (2005) has argued that there is a 'double dividend' in consuming differently while reducing our environmental impact, recalling the 'Factor Four' (doubling wealth, halving resource use) proposals to increase efficiency by Amory Lovins and his colleagues at the Rocky Mountain Institute (Von Weizsäcker, Lovins & Lovins 1997).

This is not the place to detail possible practical approaches to sustainability. It is sufficient to note that such approaches exist (Jackson & Michaelis 2003). A bigger challenge is for them to be adopted, on a scale to influence outcomes detectably. In 1999, the

British Government (*Quality of Life Counts* 1999: 8) produced its strategy for sustainable development. It had four aims:

1. Social progress which recognizes the needs of everyone.
2. Effective protection of the environment.
3. Prudent use of natural resources.
4. Maintenance of high and stable levels of economic growth and employment.

To measure its progress towards these aims the Government identified 147 'Quality of Life' indicators, with 15 of them regarded as 'headline indicators' (economic growth, investment, employment, poverty, education, health, housing, crime, greenhouse gas emissions, air quality, road traffic, river water quality, wildlife, land use and waste); it publishes reports on progress towards (or away from) these each year. In general, the trend has been positive, although uneven (Sustainable Development Commission 2004).

Does all this have anything to do with theology? The answer becomes a very definite 'yes' as soon as we acknowledge that God has put us in this world to care for it on his behalf. Our purpose in this life is to praise our creator and sustainer both with our own mouths and lives, but also with all the rest of creation (Ps. 148). It was because God so loved the *cosmos* (the Greek word translated 'world' in John 3:16) that he gave his Son to die for us and thereby to empower us to fulfil his purpose for it. The gospel we preach must recognize that Christ has reconciled *all things* to the Father through his death on the cross (Col. 1:20). Derek Tidball (1999: 51, 60) comments:

> Paul never narrows the focus of his vision to concentrate on a few elect people who enjoy the benefits of salvation for their own good irrespective of what happens to the rest of creation. His lens is always a wide angle lens which keeps the whole of creation in view. The new creation of the church is a step in the plan of God toward the renewal of *all things* . . . What was true on a cosmic scale is also true on a personal level. So Paul applies it to the Colossian believers who, because of their faith in Christ, are already in the process of experiencing reconciliation with God.

We err if we separate the cosmic from the personal. We have an integral role in the divine strategy, because Christ's work enables us to function as God's stewards – and demands that we do so. Oliver O'Donovan (1986: 55) is in no doubt that

> the redemption of the world and of mankind does not serve merely to put us back in the Garden of Eden where we began. It leads us on to that further destiny to which, even in the Garden of Eden, we were already directed. For the creation was given to us with its own goal and purpose, so that the outcome of the world's story cannot be a cyclical return to the beginnings, but must fulfil that purpose in the freeing of creation from its 'futility' (Rom. 8:20) . . . The eschatological transformation of the world is neither the mere repetition of the created world nor its negation. It is its fulfilment, its *telos* or end.

The fact that we are made in God's image makes this possible. God's Two Books should be read together (Ps. 19). There is an unanswerable moral basis to sustainable development (and sustainable consumption) (Jones 2003).

Lynn White ended his enquiry into the 'historical roots of our ecologic crisis' by proposing Francis of Assisi as a patron saint for ecologists. René Dubos (1973: 173) has argued that Benedict with his concern for caring agriculture and countryside management would be a much better model, as 'reverence is not enough, because man has never been a passive witness of nature . . . To be creative, man . . . must read the book of external nature and the book of his own nature, to discern the common patterns and harmonies.' Donald Worster (1993: 218) has said much the same:

> It is not possible, or even desirable to try to go back to a pre-modern religious world view . . . The idea of making Franciscans of everyone in the world would be an ethnocentric and anachronistic solution to the modern dilemma . . . The only deep solution open to us is to begin transcending our fundamental world view – creating a post materialist view of ourselves and the natural world, a view that summons back some of the lost wisdom of the past but does not depend on a return to old discarded creeds.

I began with John Taylor's *Enough Is Enough*. Taylor (1975: 101) found hope in 'the enormous number of people of all ages and in many different countries who have come to the conclusion that unless we can discover a radically new style of living and can put it into practice, the delicate balance of life on this planet will be irretrievably deranged and we shall be plunged into chaos'. John Stott (1977: 29) commented on this conclusion:

> Instead of being always one of the chief bastions of the *status quo*, the Church is to develop a Christian counter-culture with its own distinctive goals, values, standards and lifestyle, a realistic alternative to the contemporary technocracy which is marked by bondage, materialism, self-centredness and greed. Christ's call to obedience is a call to be different, not conformist.

That is the message of this book. Christians should be showing how to find, encourage and maintain sustainability as part of their discipleship. Creation care is not an option for zealots; it is an integral part of our obedience to Christ and our witness to the world. We need courage, but we may be pushing an open door. Jonathon Porritt, Chairman of the UK Sustainability Development Commission, introduced a report on the possible contribution of faith groups to sustainable development: 'For sustainable development, what motivates us is critical . . . [W]e constantly underestimate the hunger for transcendence, just as we underestimate our extraordinary capacity for the deepest feelings of empathy and compassion for other people and for the living world' (Porritt 2006: 5). The report concluded that 'faith groups' 'have much to offer in helping to deliver sustainable development . . . Prayer and spiritual belief offer a means of support lacking in the secular world' (9).

We need to boldly go and challenge the prevalent 'hostility to those who promote a spiritually inspired perspective on today's sustainable development challenges' (Porritt 2005: 300). Listing the most common misconceptions about global warming, Al Gore identifies the worst misconception of all as 'There is nothing we can do.' He lists many things we can do – but he is unequivocal: 'we need to start now' (Gore 2006: 315).

© R. J. Berry, 2007

2. TOWARDS A THEOLOGY OF SUSTAINABILITY

Dave Bookless

The Revd Dave Bookless is National Director of A Rocha UK (www.arocha.org), and based in multiracial Southall, west London. Ordained in 1991, he served in two Southall parishes before leaving to found A Rocha UK in 2001, jointly with his wife, Anne. The first major project, A Rocha Living Waterways, has seen an urban wasteland transformed into a Country Park and nature area, which A Rocha helps manage. Dave's role is now national, seeking through speaking and writing to be a Christian voice in the environmental world, and an environmental voice in the Christian world.

'Sustainability' is a concept in search of a home. Many have an idea of what it means, but scratch below the surface and the ideas are diverse at best, contradictory at worst. Sustainability has become a rallying cry, adopted by politicians, economists, multinational corporations, scientists, environmentalists, town planners and faith leaders . . . who use it to mean what they want it to mean.

This chapter tries to put sustainability in its place – to attempt to define it, by asking key questions. What are we to sustain, why, and for whom? Are we sustaining for ourselves, for future generations, for other species, for the earth itself? Why so – for self-preservation, or for broader altruistic purposes? What gives us our drive to sustain, and what gives individual species and whole ecosystems their value? What makes them worthy of being sustained? On what philosophical or ethical value system is sustainability based? As we explore these questions, we shall find that a biblical theology of sustainability is not only possible, but is arguably the most plausible and practical approach to a sustainable world.

Defining terms

It was in 1987, in preparation for the Brundtland Report *Our Common Future*, that the World Commission on Environment and Development (1987) first drafted the most widely used definition of sustainable development: 'Sustainable development seeks to meet the needs and aspirations of the present without compromising the ability to meet those of the future.'

While this is helpful in that everybody can agree to it, it is capable of endless interpretation. A simple web search reveals dozens of competing definitions, both of 'sustainability' and 'sustainable development'.[1] Here, we shall use the single word 'sustainability' rather than the more problematic concept of 'sustainable development'. In theological terms, the latter has been described by the South American liberation theologian Leonardo Boff (2003) as oxymoronic: 'a contradiction in terms and an illusion'. According to Boff, 'sustainable' implies interdependence and dynamic equilibrium, while 'development' is a Trojan Horse, carrying self-justifying Western assumptions of exploitative economic growth, which places human interests first. Whether or not one accepts Boff's thesis, it illustrates the minefield of defining such a slippery term, and as one word is easier to define than two, we shall concentrate on 'sustainability' itself.

---

1. The Global Development Research Center lists over a hundred definitions of sustainability (http://www.gdrc.org/sustdev/ definitions.html).

It is generally held that there are broadly three potential philosophical foundations for understanding the relationship of human beings to their environment (and thus to understanding sustainability): the *anthropocentric*, the *ecocentric* and the *theocentric*. In brief caricature:

- The *anthropocentric* view says that the world is here for human use and enjoyment. Sustainability is simply our responsibility to provide enough for fellow humans and for future human generations.
- The *ecocentric* view sees humans as simply one part of an interdependent biosphere, with no greater rights than any other part. We sustain for the greater good.
- The *theocentric* view sees the world (human and non-human) as deriving its value from being created and sustained by God.

From this, it can be seen immediately that the Brundtland Commission's definition of sustainability is implicitly anthropocentric – the 'needs and aspirations' of human beings are central. Similarly, and more recently, the Millennium Ecosystem Assessment (MA 2005) is self-consciously anthropocentric – perhaps in order to appeal to those politicians and businesses that will listen only to self-interest. Thus the Millennium Ecosystem Assessment describes the state of the planet in terms of those 'ecosystem services' on which *human* welfare depends. The Millennium Ecosystem Assessment's logo of planet Earth in the shape of a small house, elegantly encapsulates this anthropocentric notion of sustainability. 'Ecology' is derived from the Greek *oikos*, 'home', and this notion of sustainability is all about keeping *our* house in order for *our* sakes.

Christianity has often been seen as supporting the anthropocentric position. In Lynn White's famous words, from his influential article (1967) in *Science*, Western Christianity is 'the most anthropocentric religion the world has seen'. There is plenty of evidence to support such a view. The Swiss Reformer John Calvin (1847: 98) stated, 'the end for which all things were created [was] that none of the convenience and necessities of life might be wanting to men'. Even the patron saint of ecologists, St Francis of Assisi

(1959: 145) stated, 'Every creature proclaims: "God made me for your sake O man!"'

However, it is often forgotten that Lynn White was critiquing not Christianity per se but a Western aberration of it, and saw solutions to the problem in a rediscovery of alternative traditions within Christianity. The anthropocentrism that White identifies owes more to Greek philosophy and Renaissance humanism than the biblical tradition (Bauckham 2002). As we shall see shortly, a biblical theology of sustainability is predicated on an understanding that the world is ultimately *for* God, not for human beings. Psalm 24:1 states, 'The earth is the LORD's and everything in it'. In the New Testament, Colossians 1:16 goes further by saying that all things were created 'by' and 'for' Jesus Christ.

Ultimately the anthropocentric view is fundamentally flawed, because (1) it sees human beings as somehow above or separate from the rest of the biosphere, and because (2) it places too much faith in human endeavour to find solutions to the crises we cause. Anthropocentrism leads directly to technocentrism – faith in the ingenuity of humanity, in the progress of science and its practical applications. Historically, anthropocentrism has led inexorably to short-term self-interested use of the planet, which is seen as there for our benefit alone. We are consumers, developers and answerable only to ourselves. The great fallacy of anthropocentrism is this blind faith in humanity, a faith people today are losing fast – faced with the potential nightmares of human-caused climate change, resource depletion and profit-led genetic modification. Even within the environmental movement, the generation that put its faith in governments and individuals to change once they knew the facts is fast disappearing. The Johannesburg World Summit on Sustainable Development in 1992 was a watershed in its acknowledgment that, while we know more and more about both the crisis and the potential solutions, people don't want to change.

The second, ecocentric, view is increasingly popular, moving beyond 'alternative' and 'New Age' circles into mainstream philosophical (if not yet always scientific) thinking. Aldo Leopold (1949) was one of the first to argue for a rethinking of our relationship with nature, advocating a 'land ethic' where humans see themselves as part of, rather than apart from, ecosystems. Following on, Fritjof Capra, Thomas Berry, Arne Naess and many more have seen the need to dispense with the dominant anthropocentric model, and replace it with a more holistic, ecocentric (or geocentric) model. The environmental crisis is seen to be caused by an alienating mechanistic distancing between humans and their environment, and can be overcome, healed or regain sustainability only through an integrated and harmonious holding together of all things.

The ecocentric view is profoundly attractive to postmodern people, disillusioned with 'progress' and the empty benefits of materialism. It has taken many forms, from deep ecology, through ecofeminism to attempts by those such as Matthew Fox to create an ecocentric Christian 'creation theology'. Fox is rightly regarded by most mainstream Christians as having rejected the heart of the Christian faith – in denying the need for redemption in favour of a creation theology that emphasizes self-realization and absorption. However, orthodox biblical Christianity has more in common with an ecocentric view than is often realized. While one can search the Bible and Christian writers to find 'anthropocentric' proof texts, one can also find passages that show humans to be part of the ecosystem rather than above it, interdependent rather than independent. Genesis 2 speaks of the first human as Adam, made from *adamah*, the 'dust' or 'soil'. The majority of the Old Testament is about the interrelationship of people and place – chosen people and Promised Land. St Francis of Assisi talked of 'brother sun and sister moon', and many of the great Christian mystics drew inspiration from their encounter with the divine in and through creation. The biblical narrative shows that there is, ultimately, no theology without ecology.

Despite these positive comments, there are two major problems with an ecocentric view – one practical and the other theological.

In practical terms, the problem with an ecocentric view of sustainability is that it quickly leads to ethical dilemmas over intervention. If humans are merely one among the millions of species, with no inherent distinct value or role, what right have we to intervene in natural systems? The dilemma has been seen in two recent clashes in the British conservation world.

In the Scottish Hebridean islands, hedgehogs are not native, but their introduction – whether deliberate or careless – has caused devastation to ground-nesting birds (hedgehogs being partial to the odd omelette). On the one hand, conservationists from the RSPB have argued for a cull where hedgehogs cannot be removed humanely. On the other, animal rights campaigners and the Mrs Tiggywinkle preservation society have argued that we have no right to harm the hedgehogs. There has been a similar impasse over the ruddy duck – an American diving duck introduced to Europe that is interbreeding with and thus threatening the endangered white-headed duck, which has a small population in Iberia. If we take a step back, we can see that here we have a clash of world views regarding sustainability. Conservationists are, whether they realize it or not, operating from an assumption that human beings have a right to intervene in natural systems, an assumption that is implicitly anthropocentric or at least gives humans special powers. The animal-rights activists tend to operate from an ecocentric world view.

We are going to see these kinds of clashes increase in coming years, as the fault lines deepen between the modern largely anthropocentric science-based world that assumes human rights and abilities to adapt and intervene, and a postmodern ecocentric mentality where humans are viewed as an evolutionary anomaly that causes more harm than good to the planet. Some American philosophers have started to see humans as the virus species, the plague on the planet. These are two conflicting philosophies of sustainability: one believes humans should and can sustain the planet, while the other is characterized by a memorable sentence from Professor James Lovelock (1995: 61): 'I would sooner expect a goat to succeed as a gardener as expect humans to become stewards of the earth.'

John Stott (2000: 9) elegantly encapsulates the flaws respectively of both the ecocentric and anthropocentric positions in saying, 'We must not treat nature obsequiously as if it were God, nor behave towards it arrogantly as if we were God.' However, today, with this impasse between the two main models of sustainability (the anthropocentric and the ecocentric), there exists a great and pressing opportunity for a third model: a theocentric understanding of sustainability based on biblical principles. I propose that it is here within the Judeo-Christian tradition that the concept of sustainability most naturally finds its home, and suggest a series of theological propositions, each with ethical and practical outcomes, which can provide alternative pillars for a Christian understanding of sustainability.

The first pillar is simply that, in the final resort, sustainability is not entirely dependent on humanity, because *God is both Creator and Sustainer*. The world's faiths, despite all their varied creation myths, unite in seeing the earth as more than the product of random chance. Whether monotheistic, polytheistic or pantheistic, they attribute divinely derived value to the earth and its creatures. An increasing number are admitting that it is in fact very hard to create a workable ethic of sustainability without such a basis for valuing and stewarding nature. In an introduction to Sustainability for Columbia University's Earth Center's programme for Environmental Studies students, the 'roots of the values inherent in sustainability' are clearly traced to 'traditional value systems' such as 'eastern and aboriginal religions . . . the Judaeo-Christian ethic . . . [and] Islam'.[2]

---

2. 'Cultural Roots of the Concept of Sustainability: The concept of sustainability has roots in traditional value systems. Many Eastern and aboriginal religions emphasize the interdependency of humans and nature and grant respect and consideration to all living things. Humans are within nature, not above it. In Western societies, the Judeo-Christian ethic of wise stewardship of creation has had its place. Islam views nature as a revelation of God and gives it very high value. And regarding equity, most cultures have had something akin to the "golden rule" of doing unto others as you would have them do unto you. Accepting responsibility for future generations has even been central in some traditions, such as the Six Nations Iroquois Confederacy, who believed that "In our every deliberation, we must consider the impact of our decisions on the next seven generations." Finally, considering the economic aspect of sustainability, the prophets of every major world religion have warned against the negative effects of overconsumption or giving excessive priority to the material aspects of life' (Noble & Costa 1999; 2 Durning 1992; Coward 1995; Costa & Noble 1999).

Judeo-Christian theology is not *anthropo*centric, *eco*centric, *bio*centric or *geo*centric, but *theo*centric. It begins neither with human rights and responsibilities, nor with intrinsic natural values, but with God. In biblical terms, sustainability must begin with God both as creator and also, crucially, as sustainer. God is the one by whom all things are made, and who holds all things together – in whom all things live and move and have their being.

This is both disturbing and comforting. It is disturbing because humans dislike admitting their cosmic insignificance. We are neither the masters nor the sustainers of the universe. It is comforting because the track record of human beings is so poor. It challenges both anthropocentrism and ecocentrism. In a time of environmental despair, Christian theology offers much needed hope in the promise that ultimately God is committed to sustaining and renewing the earth.

Several key ethical imperatives flow from this understanding of God's creating and sustaining love. If the earth is God's, not ours, and if God retains oversight and involvement, then attitudes of *respect* and even *reverence* towards natural systems ensue. As Gerard Manley Hopkins put it, 'The world is charged with the grandeur of God'. Other traditions speak of the sacramental quality of all creation, the ability of natural systems to reveal the Creator and communicate the immanence of an otherwise transcendent God. Every part of creation should be respected as having intrinsic value, because it is fashioned by the creator of all. This is critical in our thinking about sustainability – without belief in a creator, it is difficult to find value in living or inanimate things apart from their instrumental value (usually expressed as their economic value) to human beings. For instance, the widely accepted model favoured by the UK government talks of three equally important aspects to sustainability: the *environmental*, the *social* and the *economic*. In practice, the economic dominates, because it provides the easiest way of measuring value; how else does one measure the value of a rainforest, or the value of a contented community? A biblical understanding of sustainability turns this on its head. Economics can never be equated with the social or environmental aspects of sustainability; it is merely a servant of the other two. Wealth and money are only tools for the service of society, and should have no value independent of the greater good they create. In the context of environmental sustainability, money and the human economy should be set within the wider context of the earth. True value lies not in measurable monetary wealth, nor in usefulness to human beings, but is intrinsic to being created by God. Thus every object and every creature must be respected, not simply as resources, but as unique repositories of God's wisdom.

Belief in God's sustaining involvement also leads to an ethical attitude of *restraint*. We should exercise great caution in our intervention in natural systems, respect the natural wisdom of the Creator, and observe the ability of nature to adapt to changing circumstances without human interference. Furthermore, the biblical understanding of sabbath is linked to the need for both *restraint* and *rest*, and is crucial to understanding God as creator and sustainer. The sabbath is a creation ordinance (a rest for God and for all creation) interpreted in the Torah as a rest for farm animals and for the land itself, as much as for people.

So, the first pillar of a Christian theology of sustainability is that *God is creator and sustainer*. At this point, the critic of Christianity will tend to chip in, 'If God is the sustainer, does not that allow human beings off the hook? Does it not encourage the myth that God is in charge, so we can do what we like (exploit, destroy, live unsustainably), knowing that he will sort it all out in the end?' Good question. Poor theology.

The second pillar of a biblical theology of sustainability is that of *covenantal stewardship*. Although some environmentalists have criticized the term 'stewardship' in recent years, a true understanding of it is integral to the essence of sustainability. Stewardship implies looking after somebody else's property on their behalf. Biblical stewardship understands that the earth is God's, not ours, removing any 'rights' to use its resources without constraint. It also contains the vital notions of responsibility and accountability: stewards have to answer to the owner. Biblical stewardship is also within the context of covenant: a contractual and binding agreement between God, people and land. The creation covenant of Genesis 9, with the sign of the rainbow, conveys God's commitment to the whole earth and every living creature within it, a commitment not to destroy the earth by flood again, no matter how bad things get, and thus a commitment to sustain creation.

The human responsibility to rule over creation, given in Genesis 1:26–28, belongs within this covenantal context. The world is God's, by creation, ownership and sustenance. Humans are given the sacred trust of being God's stewards, or tenant trustees. Summarized in Genesis 2:15, the invitation to 'till and keep' the garden is the heart of a practical Christian understanding of sustainable stewardship. *Tilling* is about working responsibly, and includes all human endeavour in managing the earth and using natural resources. It encompasses farming, animal husbandry, forestry, mining and resource extraction, hunting, fishing and industry. *Keeping* is about doing all of this in a way that today we would call sustainable: it is about restraint and respect, never taking from natural systems beyond their capacity to renew and replace. It is about conservation, not as a way of attempting to preserve a system in formaldehyde, but as dynamic engagement with an ecosystem, seeking to maximize fruitfulness, both in terms of yield and biodiversity. And, crucially, both tilling and keeping are implicitly dependent upon good science, science that is not about treating the earth as a laboratory for value-free experimentation, but science as the reverent exploration of God's book of works, recording and studying natural systems in order to understand our effect upon them, to maximize yields but always in such a way as to leave enough for other species and future generations. Thus the pillar of covenantal stewardship leads to ethical values such as *responsibility* (the duties of trusteeship, to maintain, conserve and also creatively develop a property), and delegated *rule* (an authority that is not absolute or random but contingent on the contract between owner and steward).

The Old Testament, seen by several recent theologians as primarily a story of the three-way relationship between people, God and land (or natural environment), gives many examples of how this motif of covenantal stewardship is worked out in sustainable living. One of many, but one of the most vivid, comes in Deuteronomy 22:6–7, where the people of Israel are told what to do if they find a ground-nesting bird in their field. They are permitted to eat the eggs or chicks, but commanded to leave the mother bird – so she may of course nest again. It is a brilliantly simple example of sustainable use of the natural world. As Steven Bouma-Prediger (2001: 149–150) puts it:

> We are permitted to use the fruit of the earth, but we are not allowed to destroy the earth's ability to be fruitful . . . Creatures provide sustenance for others and reproduce themselves. In this interdependent world of cycles and systems, even the most 'unimportant' species and 'ugly' creatures are valuable. From this theological motif I derive the ethical principle of sustainability. We dare not deplete or permanently damage that which supports, maintains, and nourishes our every existence. Nor ought we needlessly or wantonly impair the ability of other creatures to sustain themselves.

Alongside the pillar of covenantal stewardship (with the awesome power and responsibility that gives to human beings) is a third pillar, which I describe as the *creation–fall–redemption* paradigm. It is the classic Christian analysis of both the human condition and the state of the planet. At its simplest it is three short statements:

1. God made a good world.
2. Human moral failure causes a breakdown in the relationships between God, people and all creation.
3. God in Christ provides hope for humanity and for the whole material creation.

Now, each of those short statements contains a mass of theological assumptions, but let's keep it simple. The concept of sustainability has arisen at a time when the world is under immense threat from human carelessness and abuse. Within the concept of sustainability are assumptions that parallel the basic diagnosis, prognosis and treatment of classic Christian theology:

1. The world is worth sustaining: it has value and goodness.
2. Humanity has spoiled its good home, threatening our very future.

3. It is worth doing something about this: a sustainable future is
   achievable.

I suggest that these assumptions underwrite the very concept of
sustainability and that they make sense only within a theocentric
world view. The Judeo-Christian tradition is based around the
attempt to answer the ultimate question of how we put right what
has gone wrong, with ourselves and with the world around us.
Biblical Christianity's radical claim (and that which differentiates it
from other world faiths) is that we cannot do this ourselves – no
amount of rebuilding can ever put Humpty Dumpty together
again. We are thrown instead on the mercy of God, a God who in
Christ enters the created material world and through his death and
resurrection enables all that is broken to be restored.

This paradigm of creation, fall and redemption is seen in the
first nine chapters of Genesis: a world God declares good and a
perfect garden inhabited by innocent people are spoiled through
human selfishness. The result is a breakdown in relationships
between God, people and planet; the earth itself is cursed in
Genesis 3 as a result. However, the Noahic story of Genesis 6–9
brings God's rescue and restoration of representatives of every
living creature upon the earth, not just of people. Similarly, in the
New Testament the ministry of Christ assumes creation has
enough of God's goodness remaining within it to be the source of
most of Jesus' stories and parables. The death and resurrection of
Christ are also clearly put within the cosmic context of reconciliation and restoration, as passages such as Romans 8 and Colossians
1 amply demonstrate.

The ethical and practical implications of all this for our thinking
on sustainability are immense. We live at a time of crisis in
the global environmental movement. It is more than anything
else a crisis of hope. In an influential paper, 'The Death of
Environmentalism', Michael Shellenberger and Ted Nordhaus
(2004: 7) wrote, 'What the environmental movement needs more
than anything else right now is to take a collective step back to re-
think everything. We shall never be able to turn things around as
long as we understand our failures as essentially tactical and make
proposals that are essentially technical.' Later in the same article

they state, 'Environmentalists need to tap into the creative worlds of myth-making, even religion, not to better sell narrow and technical policy proposals but rather to figure out who we are and who we need to be' (34).

Sustainability is dependent on hope. Without it, there is no point in struggling to sustain the unsustainable. The Christian paradigm of a world created good, spoiled by humanity, but redeemed by God in Christ offers a hope wider than human activity and that also compels human beings to respond in hopeful action. Because of Christ we have hope for the world, and can live and act hopefully.

For Christians, two further, closely connected pillars on which this understanding of sustainability depends are those of *bodily resurrection* and *new creation*. The resurrection of Jesus Christ, as N. T. Wright amply demonstrates in his magisterial *The Resurrection of the Son of God* (2003), is crucial to understanding our future and that of the whole material universe. A bodily resurrection, combining the healed scars of a fallen world with the perfection of eternity, is a model for understanding the future reality of all God wishes to rescue and restore. The new creation, or new heavens and new earth, of which Christ's body is the first fruits, is a material world, not a spiritualized other-worldly escape, but the earthing of heaven – when God's home will be with humankind. From Isaiah to Revelation the images are of a restored ecosystem, which includes non-human as well as human elements: lions, lambs, snakes and trees. All that is good and true and unspoiled in the natural world, and also in the world of human creativity will be brought into this new world. The original Garden of Eden becomes the garden city of Revelation, a city like no current earthly one, because it is a vision of eternal sustainability.

All of this may seem a long way from saving threatened frogs, recycling more effectively, or campaigning to tackle climate change, but it is crucial, because it is about what causes people to live and act hopefully. Richard Bauckham and Trevor Hart (1999: 82) argue that 'Christianity is a faith which is essentially forward looking and forward moving, orientated towards and living now ever in the light cast backwards by God's promised future.' In other words, our hopeful vision of God's future enables us to work for sustainability today. Thus there is an imperative for Christians to be involved in practical expressions of sustainable living, and to campaign for a more sustainable world. Bauckham and Hart describe Christian projects that seek to embody this vision as 'scattered acts of recreative anticipation of God's promised future' (1999: 71). Elsewhere they have been described as 'small scale acts of resistance' (Downham 2005), resistance to the self-serving materialism of modern Western lifestyles.

This Christian understanding of the scope and certainty of God's purposes for the created order leads not to a crisis-driven panic, vainly trying to stop the juggernaut of Western civilization by throwing ourselves under its wheels, nor to an unrealistic faith in technical human ability to solve all our problems, but to patient, good-quality science, done humbly and reverently, to practical and often radical lifestyle changes undertaken joyfully and worshipfully, and to conservation action that demonstrates God's love for all creation. It will be characterized by

- *integrity*: because all we do is in response to God, and we are answerable to him for the quality of our work;
- *incarnation*: the costly long-term, usually unglamorous identification of people with a particular place and community;
- *integration*: getting beyond the senseless divide between development and conservation in seeing the big picture – that God cares for all he has made.

Most of all, as with all realistic models of sustainability, it will be characterized by a humble acceptance of the human privilege and duty to act as caretakers of God's world. Today's global environmental crisis is caused by one species: the human species. And the crisis of confidence in the environmental movement is due to the intransigent and myopic selfishness of the same species. We should not be surprised that the Director General of the World Conservation Union, Achim Steiner, argues that 90% of conservation work needs to be not with wildlife, but with people (personal communication). People are the problem, but they also (under God) hold the key to the solution. Bill Bryson (2004: 572), in his entertaining and wide-ranging *A Short History of Nearly Everything*, concludes:

> If you were designing an organism to look after life in our lonely cosmos, to monitor where it is going, and keep a record of where it has been, you wouldn't choose human beings for the job. But here's an extremely salient point – we have been chosen, by fate or providence or whatever you wish to call it. As far as we can tell, we are the best there is.

Bryson comes precious close here to repeating the Genesis mandate that God entrusts to humans. As an agnostic, it leaves him (and many others) pretty nervous of the future. If history is anything to go on, would *you* trust human beings with sustaining the earth? Yet, with Christian hope, we can humbly but confidently take on this mandate. We trust not in ourselves but in God for the ultimate future, and we work now to live in the light of that future and create signs that point to it.

To return to where we began, if sustainability is a concept in search of a home, then a Christian world view is a natural home for it. J. Baird Caldicott, not himself a Christian, has admitted that Christianity 'exquisitely matches the requirements of conservation biology. It confers objective value on nature in the clearest and most unambiguous of ways: by divine decree' (quoted in Harris 2005). As Christians we should have a *holistic* world view (neither anthropocentric nor ecocentric, but theocentric), a *realistic* world view (taking into account the full range of possible human effects on the planet – from devastation to enhancement), and a *hopeful* world view (believing that the earth is not only safe in God's hands, but that all creation is being and will be made new in Christ). If this is what we believe, and if we begin to live it out in practical expression of Christian hope, then I believe we could see a major impact both on the environmental and Christian worlds.

3. THE CHALLENGE OF SUSTAINABILITY

John Houghton

Sir John Houghton, CBE, FRS, is a former Professor of Atmospheric Physics at Oxford University. He was Director-General of the UK Meteorological Office (1983–91). He served as Chairman of the Royal Commission in Environmental Pollution (1992–8) and chaired the Scientific Panel of the Intergovernmental Panel on Climate Change from its inception in 1988 until 2002. In 2006 he was awarded the Japan Prize 'for his pioneering research on atmospheric structure and composition, based on his satellite observation technology and his promotion of international assessments of climate change'. He currently chairs the John Ray Initiative (www.jri.org.uk) and is President of the Victoria Institute. He is the author of Does God Play Dice? *(IVP, 1988),* The Search for God: Can Science Help? *(Lion, 1995) and* Global Warming: The Complete Briefing *(Cambridge University Press, 3rd ed., 2004). This chapter is a revised version of Sir John's Presidential Address to the Victoria Institute given at a joint meeting of the Institute with Christians in Science and the John Ray Initiative on 1 October 2005.*

Imagine you are a member of the crew of a large spaceship on a voyage to visit a distant planet. Your journey there and back will take many years. An adequate, high-quality, source of energy is readily available in the radiation from the sun. Otherwise, resources for the journey are limited. The crew on the spacecraft are engaged in managing their resources as carefully as possible. A local biosphere is created in the spacecraft where plants are grown for food and everything is recycled. Careful accounts are kept of all resources, with especial emphasis on non-replaceable components. That the resources be *sustainable* at least for the duration of the voyage, both there and back, is clearly essential.

Planet Earth is enormously larger than such a spaceship. The crew of Spaceship Earth is also enormously larger – six billion and rising. But the principle of sustainability needs to be applied to Spaceship Earth as rigorously as it has to be applied to the much smaller vehicle on an interplanetary journey. The first person to use the term 'Spaceship Earth' seems to have been Buckminster Fuller (1963), but it was taken up and introduced into rigorous analysis by Kenneth Boulding, a distinguished American economist. He contrasted an 'open' or 'cowboy' economy (as he called an unconstrained economy) with a 'spaceship' economy in which sustainability is paramount (Boulding 1966).

Sustainability is an idea that concerns activities and communities as well as physical resources. I am mainly concerned here with the sustainability of resources and of our environment, but it is increasingly important to realize that environmental sustainability cannot legitimately be separated from social sustainability (and sustainable communities) and sustainable economics. *Sustainable Development* provides an all-embracing term; the Brundtland Report, *Our Common Future* (World Commission on Environment and Development 1987), provides a milestone review of sustainable development issues.

There have been many definitions of sustainability. The simplest I know is 'not cheating on our children'. To that may be added 'not cheating on our neighbours' and 'not cheating on the rest of creation'. In other words, not passing on to our children or any future generation an Earth that is degraded compared to the one we inherited, and also sharing common resources as necessary with our neighbours in the rest of the world and caring properly for the non-human creation.

Crisis of sustainability

It is generally accepted that the human activities of an increasing world population – now at 6 billion – together with rapid industrial development are leading to serious environmental damage on a very large scale. Notwithstanding, some still deny that degradation is happening; others deny that degradation matters. Scientists have an important role in ensuring the availability of accurate information and also in pointing to how humans can begin to solve the problems.

Many things are happening in our modern world that are just not sustainable (see the United Nations Environmental Programme 2002). In fact, we are all guilty of cheating in the three respects I have mentioned: see the table below. The table lists five of the most important environmental issues, indicating how they are all connected and also linked to other major areas of human activity or concern. Take deforestation: every year an area of tropical forest approximately equal to that of Ireland is cut down or burnt. Some of this is to harvest valuable hardwoods (albeit unsustainably); some is to clear forest in order to raise beef cattle for some of the world's richest countries. This level of deforestation adds significantly to the atmospheric greenhouse gases carbon dioxide and methane, so increasing the rate of human-induced climate change. It is also likely to change the local climate close to the

Table: Important sustainability issues

Issue	*Linked to*
Global warming and climate change	Energy, transport, biodiversity loss, deforestation
Land-use change	Biodiversity loss, deforestation, climate change, soil loss, agriculture, water
Consumption	Waste, fish, food, energy, transport, deforestation, water
Waste	Consumption, energy, agriculture, food
Fishing	Consumption, food

region where the deforestation is occurring: if current levels of deforestation continue in the Amazon, some of Amazonia could become much drier, even semi-desert, during this century. Further, when the trees go, soil is lost by erosion; again in many parts of Amazonia the soil is poor and easily washed away. Tropical forests are also rich in biodiversity. With loss of forests there will be much irreplaceable biodiversity loss.

All these issues present enormous challenges. My concern here is to address in some detail the issue with which I have been most concerned, namely that of global warming and climate change, explaining the essential roles of both science and faith in getting to grips with it.

Global warming and climate change

In the early twentieth century, the French painter Claude Monet spent time in London and painted wonderful pictures of the light coming through the smog. London was blighted by *local pollution* – from domestic and industrial chimneys around London itself. Thanks to the Clean Air Acts beginning in the 1950s, those awful smogs now belong to the past, although London's atmosphere could be still cleaner. Global Warming and Climate Change is about *global pollution*, emissions of invisible gases such as carbon dioxide that spread around the whole atmosphere and affect everybody. Global pollution requires global solutions. To different extents, we are all contributing to this global pollution.

For a comprehensive account of the science, impacts, policy and economics issues of climate change, see Intergovernmental Panel on Climate Change (2001); briefer reviews are in Houghton 2004, 2005. In summary, by absorbing infra-red or 'heat' radiation from the earth's surface, 'greenhouse gases' such as water vapour and carbon dioxide act as blankets over the earth's surface, keeping it warmer than it would otherwise be. The existence of this natural 'greenhouse effect' has been known from the early nineteenth century; it is essential to the provision of our current climate to which ecosystems and we humans have adapted.

Since the beginning of the Industrial Revolution around 1750, one of these greenhouse gases, carbon dioxide, has increased by over 30% and is now at a higher concentration in the atmosphere than for at least half a million years. Chemical analysis shows that this increase is due largely to the burning of fossil fuels (coal, oil and gas), about one-third coming each from the industrial, buildings and transport sectors. If no action is taken to curb these emissions, the carbon dioxide concentration will rise during the twenty-first century to two or three times its pre-industrial level. Human activities have led also to a doubling in the atmosphere of the amount of methane, also a greenhouse gas (although less important than carbon dioxide because of its lower amounts) since 1760.

The climate record over past centuries shows a lot of natural variability. The rise in global average temperature of about 0.7°C (and its rate of rise) during the twentieth century is well outside the range of known natural variability, even that shown in the 'medieval warm period' around 1300 and the 'little ice age' around the period 1600–1800. The year 1998 was the warmest year in the instrumental record and, even more striking, each of the first eight months of 1998 was the warmest on record for that month. There is strong evidence that most of the warming since the 1960s is due to the increase of greenhouse gases, especially carbon dioxide. This is supported by observations on the warming of the oceans.

Over the twenty-first century the global average temperature is projected to rise by between 2° and 6°C (3.5° to 11°F) from its pre-industrial level; the range represents different assumptions about emissions of greenhouse gases and about the sensitivity of the climate model used in making the estimate. For *global average* temperature, a rise of this amount is large. The difference between the middle of an ice age and the warm periods in between is only about 5° or 6°C (9° to 11°F). So, associated with the likely warming in the twenty-first century will be a rate of change of climate equivalent to, say, half an ice age in less than a hundred years – a larger rate of change than for at least ten thousand years. Adapting to this will be difficult for both humans and many ecosystems.

The impacts of climate change

Talking in terms of changes of global average temperature, however, tells us rather little about the effects of global warming on human communities (for a well-illustrated description, see Gore 2006). Some of the most obvious impacts will be due to the rise in sea level that will occur as ocean water warms and so expands. The projected rise is of the order of half a metre (20 in.) a century and will continue for many centuries (to warm the deep oceans as well as the surface waters takes a long time). This will cause critical problems for human communities living in low-lying regions. Many areas, for instance in Bangladesh (where about ten million live within the 1 m contour), southern China, islands in the Indian and Pacific oceans, and similar such places will be impossible to protect and many millions will be displaced.

There will also be impacts from extreme events. The extremely unusual high temperatures in central Europe during the summer of 2003 led to the deaths of over twenty thousand people. Careful analysis leads to the probability that such summers are likely to be average by the middle of the twenty-first century and will be below average by 2100.

Water is becoming an increasingly important resource. A warmer world will lead to more evaporation of water from the surface, more water vapour in the atmosphere and more precipitation on average. Of greater importance is the fact that the increased condensation of water vapour in cloud formation leads to increase in the latent heat of condensation being released. Since this latent heat release is the largest source of energy driving the atmosphere's circulation, the hydrological cycle will become more intense. This means a tendency to more extreme rainfall events and also less rainfall in some semi-arid areas. The most recent estimates indicate by 2050 a typical increase in many places of around a factor of five in the risk of the most extreme floods and droughts (for floods in Europe, see Palmer & Raisanen 2002; for global extreme droughts, Burke, Brown & Christidis, in the press). Since, on average, floods and droughts are the most damaging of the world's disasters, their greater frequency and intensity is bad news for most human communities and especially for regions such as South-East Asia and sub-Saharan Africa, where such events already occur only too frequently. It is these sorts of events that provide some credence to the comparison of climate with weapons of mass destruction.

Sea-level rise, changes in water availability and extreme events will lead to increasing pressure from environmental refugees. A careful estimate has suggested that by 2050 there could be more than 150 million extra refugees due to climate change (Myers & Kent 1995).

In addition to the impacts summarized above are changes about which there is less certainty, but that would be highly damaging and possibly irreversible if they occurred. For instance, large changes are being observed in polar regions. If the temperature rises more than about 3°C (5°F) in the area of Greenland, it is estimated that meltdown of the ice cap would begin. Complete meltdown is likely to take a thousand years or more but it would add seven metres (23 ft) to the sea level.

A further concern is the thermo-haline circulation (THC – a circulation in the deep oceans, partially driven by water that has moved in the Gulf Stream from the tropics to the region between Greenland and Scandinavia). Because of evaporation on the way, the water is not only cold but salty, and hence of higher density than the surrounding water. It therefore tends to sink and provides the source for a slow circulation at low levels that connects all the oceans. This sinking assists in maintaining the Gulf Stream itself. In a globally warmed world, increased precipitation together with fresh water from melting ice will decrease the water's salinity, making it less likely to sink. The circulation would therefore weaken and possibly even stop, leading to large regional changes of climate. Evidence from palaeo-climatic history shows that such cut-off has occurred at times in the past. It is such an event that is behind the highly speculative happenings in the 2004 film Roland Emmerich directed, *The Day after Tomorrow.*

I have described adverse impacts of climate change. It is reasonable to ask if there are likely to be positive effects. There will certainly be some. Winters will be less cold and growing seasons longer in Siberia and other areas at high northern latitudes. Also, increased concentrations of carbon dioxide have a fertilizing effect on some plants and crops, which, given adequate supplies of water and nutrients, will lead to increased crop yields, probably most notably in northern mid-latitudes. However, careful studies demonstrate that adverse impacts will far outweigh positive effects, the more so as temperatures rise more than 1° or 2°C (2° to 3.5°F) above pre-industrial values.

Can we believe the evidence?

How sure are we about the scientific story? The world scientific community has carried out the most thorough assessments of the science and likely impacts of human-induced climate change through the work of the Intergovernmental Panel on Climate Change (IPCC), formed jointly by the World Meteorological Organization and the United Nations Environment Programme in 1988. I had the privilege of being chairman of the Panel's scientific assessment from 1988 to 2002. In its reports, the IPCC honestly and objectively distinguished what is reasonably well known and understood from uncertain areas. No assessments on any other scientific topic have ever been so thoroughly researched and reviewed. The Academies of Science of the world's eleven most important countries (the G8 plus India, China and Brazil) in June 2005 issued a statement endorsing the IPCC's conclusions (see the Royal Society website, www.royalsoc.ac.uk). The account I have presented here is largely based on the IPCC's reports.

Unfortunately, strong vested interests have spent tens of millions of dollars on spreading misinformation about the climate change issue. First they tried to deny the existence of any scientific evidence for rapid climate change due to human activities. More recently they have been forced to accept the fact of anthropogenic climate change but argue its impacts will not be great, that we can 'wait and see', and in any case we can always 'fix' the problem if it turns out to be substantial. The scientific evidence cannot support such arguments.

International action

International action regarding climate change began in 1992 with the establishment of the Framework Convention on Climate Change (FCCC) at the Earth Summit at Rio de Janeiro in 1992 – agreed by over 160 countries. Article 2 of the FCCC states its objective is 'to stabilize greenhouse gas concentrations in the atmosphere at a level that does not cause dangerous interference with the climate system' and 'within a time frame sufficient to allow ecosystems to adapt naturally to climate change, to ensure that food production is not threatened, and to allow economic development to proceed in a sustainable manner'. Such stabilization would also eventually stop further climate change. However, because of the long-time carbon dioxide stays in the atmosphere, the lag in the response of the climate to changes in greenhouse gases (largely due to the time oceans take to warm) and the time taken for appropriate human action to be agreed, the achievement of such stabilization will take at least the best part of a century.

Global emissions of carbon dioxide to the atmosphere from fossil fuel burning are currently approaching seven billion tonnes of carbon per annum and rising rapidly. Unless strong measures are taken they will reach two or three times their present levels during the twenty-first century and stabilization of greenhouse gas concentrations and climate will be nowhere in sight. To stabilize carbon dioxide concentrations, twenty-first century emissions must reduce to a fraction of their present levels before the century's end.

Such reductions in emissions must be made globally; all nations must take part. However, there are very large differences between carbon dioxide emissions from different countries. Expressed in tonnes of carbon per capita per annum, they vary from about 5.5 for the USA, 2.2 for Europe, 0.7 for China and 0.2 for India. The global average per capita, currently about one tonne per annum, must fall substantially, not only to enable stabilization of carbon dioxide concentration but also to allow for the expected increase in human population during the twenty-first century. Ways that are both realistic and equitable must be found to achieve the large reductions required.

The Kyoto Protocol set up by the FCCC represents a beginning for the process of greenhouse gas reduction, averaging about 5% below 1990 levels by 2012 by those developed countries that have ratified the protocol (the USA is the main country that has failed to ratify). It is an important start and shows the achievement of a

useful measure of international agreement on such a complex
issue. It also introduces for the first time international trading of
greenhouse gas emissions so that reductions can be achieved in
the most cost-effective ways.

After the Kyoto reductions by 2012, it is essential that all countries join in the agreements. The UK government has taken a lead
on this issue and has agreed a target for the reduction of greenhouse gas emissions of 60% by 2050 – predicated on a
stabilization target of doubled carbon dioxide concentrations
together with a recognition that developed countries will need to
make greater reductions to allow some headroom for developing
countries. A recent review of the economies of climate change
commissioned by the UK government (Stern 2006) has estimated
the annual costs of stabilization of carbon dioxide concentration
to be around 1% of world GDP. This can be compared with the
cost, also estimated in the Stern Review, of the damage from
climate change of up to 10% of world GDP (much more in some
developing countries) if no action is taken.

What actions can be taken?

Three sorts of actions are required if such reductions are to be
achieved.[1] First, there is energy efficiency. Approximately one-
third of energy is used in buildings (domestic and commercial),
one-third in transport and one-third by industry. Large savings can
be made in all three sectors, many with significant savings in cost.
Take buildings, for example. Recent projects such as BedZED in
South London demonstrate that 'zero emission' buildings are a
possibility (ZED = Zero Emissions Development); necessary
energy can be derived from renewable sources. Initial costs are a
little larger than for conventional buildings but the running costs a
lot less. In the transport sector, hybrid vehicles and fuel cell technology promise substantial fuel savings. Aviation, however,

---

1. For more information about energy futures, see my Prince Philip Lecture
to the Royal Society of Arts, May 2005, entitled 'Climate Change and
Sustainable Energy', available on the John Ray Initiative website
(www.jri.org.uk).

continues to grow unsustainably and economic measures, such as taxation on aviation fuel, urgently need to be applied. Within the industrial sector many companies are making serious drives for energy savings, not least because it reduces their costs.

Secondly, a wide variety of non-fossil fuels are available for development and exploitation; for instance, biomass (including waste), solar power (both photovoltaic and thermal), hydro, wind, wave, tidal and geothermal energy. These need to be developed as rapidly as possible so as to provide for energy needs in the long term. In the medium term, a contribution from nuclear energy, also largely fossil free, will probably need to be maintained.

Thirdly, there are possibilities for sequestering carbon that would otherwise enter the atmosphere, either through the planting of forests or by underground storage (e.g. in spent oil and gas wells).

The opportunities for industry for innovation, development and investment in all these areas is large.

Despite all this, many argue we should 'wait and see' before action is necessary. That is not a responsible position. The need for action is urgent for three reasons:

1. *Scientific*: because the oceans take time to warm, there is a lag in the response of climate to increasing greenhouse gases. Because of greenhouse gas emissions to date, substantial change will inevitably take place, much of which will not be realized for thirty to fifty years (Hansen et al. 2005). Further emissions just add to those changes.

2. *Economic*: energy infrastructure, for instance in power stations, also lasts typically for thirty to fifty years. It is far more cost effective to begin to phase in the required infrastructure changes now than to make them far more rapidly later.

3. *Political*: countries like China and India are industrializing very rapidly. I heard a senior energy adviser to the Chinese government say recently that China would begin to move to non-fossil-fuel sources only when the developed nations of the West take action; they will follow, not lead. China is building new electricity generating capacity of about a one gigawatt power station per week. If we want to provide an example of effective leadership, we must start now.

Science and technology

Science and technology are widely seen as *the* solutions to many of our environmental problems; for instance, by helping to mitigate human-induced climate change by providing fossil-free energy sources. Some argue simplistically that technology on its own will provide. We are told, 'The three solutions are Technology, Technology and Technology' or 'Leave it to the market and it will provide in due course.' Although science and technology are tools, the most powerful we possess, they must not be put in the role of masters. Solutions need to be much more carefully crafted than these tools can provide on their own. A long-term strategy for addressing the problem of mitigating climate change is required. It has to be internationally developed and agreed (all nations are involved); the economy and the environment have to be considered together (environmental costs need to be internalized within the economy); social and quality-of-life values have to be properly taken into account, as has energy security (too much reliance on politically vulnerable fuel sources could lead to dangerous crises).

Moreover, technology has to be appropriate to the situation in which it is deployed. This can be established only through thorough analysis. For instance, a large challenge for the government of China is how to stem the increasing flow of population from rural areas to the cities. One way would be to provide easily available energy (electricity and heating) through small-scale plants in local areas, rather than building only very large plants to provide primarily for high densities of people.

For science and technology to contribute effectively to environmental sustainability, they need to be properly integrated with social and policy considerations. Perspectives from both the natural and social sciences need to be integrated holistically so we can understand better the dynamic interplay by which environment shapes society and society in turn reshapes environment (Lawton, in the press). Scientists and technologists need humility as they apply their skills. And scientists must both learn to identify problems and seek for and propose solutions.

When talking to scientists and technologists about tackling problems of sustainability, I often emphasize the three qualities of *honesty* (especially accuracy and balance in the presentation of results), *humility* and *holism*, three Hs, an alliteration that assists in keeping them all in mind.

Technology transfer from developed to developing countries is also vital if energy growth in developing countries is going to proceed in a sustainable way. There are large opportunities for generating energy from readily available waste material (see below). Solar energy schemes can be highly versatile in size or application. Small solar systems can bring electricity in home-sized packages to villages in the developing world – again with enormous benefits to local communities. At the other end of the size scale, large solar thermal or photovoltaic projects are being envisaged that couple electricity and hydrogen generation with desalination in desert regions where water is a scarce resource.

Stewards of creation: a Christian challenge

People often tell me I am wasting my time talking about environmental sustainability. 'The world', they say, 'will never agree to take the necessary action.' I reply that I am optimistic for three reasons. First, I have experienced the commitment of the world's scientific community (including scientists from many different nations, backgrounds and cultures) in painstakingly and honestly working together to understand the problems and assessing what needs to be done. Secondly, I believe the necessary technology is available for achieving satisfactory solutions. My third reason is that I believe we have a God-given task of being good stewards of creation (John Ray Initiative 1995; Northcott 1996; Berry 2006).

Let me say more about what Christian stewardship of creation means. In the early part of Genesis, we learn that humans, made in God's image, are given the mandate to exercise stewardship/management care over the earth and its creatures (Gen. 1:26, 28; 2:15). To expand on what this means, I quote from an unpublished document, 'A Biblical Vision for Creation Care', developed following a meeting of Christian leaders at Sandy Cove, Maryland, USA, held in June 2004:

According to Scripture only human beings were made in the divine image (Gen. 1:26–27). This has sometimes been taken to mean that we are superior and are thus free to lord it over all other creatures. What it should be taken to mean is that we resemble God in some unique ways, such as our rational, moral, relational, and creative capacity. It also points to our unique ability to image God's loving care for the world and to relate intimately to God. And it certainly points to our unique planetary responsibility. The same pattern holds true in all positions of high status or relationships of power, whether in family life, education, the church, or the state. Unique capacity and unique power and unique access create unique responsibility. Being made in God's image is primarily a mandate to serve the rest of creation (Mk 10:42–45).

Only in recent decades have human beings developed the technological capacity to assess the ecological health of creation as a whole. Because we can understand the global environmental situation more thoroughly than ever before, we are in a sense better positioned to fulfil the stewardship mandate of Genesis 1 and 2 than ever before. Tragically, however, this capacity arrives several centuries after we developed the power to do great damage to the creation. We are making progress in healing some aspects of the degraded creation, but are dealing with decades of damage, and the prospect of long-lasting effects even under best-case scenarios.

We cannot hide behind the doctrine that our earth will not last or has no future. Jesus has promised to return to earth – an earth redeemed and transformed (Wright 1999a). In the meantime the earth awaits, subject to frustration, that final redemption (Rom. 8:20–22). Our task is to obey the clear injunction of Jesus to be responsible and just stewards until his return (Luke 12:41–48). Exercising this role of stewards provides an important part of our fulfilment as humans. In our modern world we concentrate so much on economic goals – getting rich and powerful. Stewardship or long-term care for our planet and its resources brings to the fore moral and spiritual goals. Reaching out for such goals could lead to nations and peoples working together more effectively and closely than is possible with many of the other goals on offer.

Aiming at goals

To make progress towards sustainability we need goals or targets to aim at. Every commercial company understands the importance of targets for successful business. Targets are needed at all levels of society – international, national, local and personal. Often, there is a reluctance to agree or set targets. A common plea is, 'Can we not achieve what is necessary by voluntary action?' Although voluntary action has achieved a few successes, in general, it fails badly to bring about change on anything like the scale required.

There are many examples of international targets that have been agreed. Within the UN Framework Convention on Climate Change (FCCC), targets for reductions of greenhouse gas concentrations in some developed countries by 2012 are set within the Kyoto Protocol. Discussions are beginning about internationally agreed targets for later dates that need to involve all major countries. In the meantime, some countries or states (e.g. the UK and California) have set real or aspirational targets of their own.[2]

At the World Summit on Sustainable Development in Johannesburg in 2002, other targets were established; for example, to halve the proportion of people without access to clean water and basic sanitation by 2015; to use and produce chemicals in ways that do not lead to significant adverse effects on human health and the environment by 2020; to maintain or restore depleted fish stocks to levels that can produce the maximum sustainable yield on an urgent basis, where possible by 2015; to achieve a significant reduction in the current rate of loss of biological diversity by 2010. Many felt these targets were too vague or too weak. But at least they have provided something to aim at.

Nationally, environmental standards, of which there are many (e.g. for use and disposal of toxic chemicals; for waste disposal and recycling), are examples of targets, some of which can be considered adequate and others (e.g. for air pollution) need to be substantially strengthened. Targets are lacking in other areas; for

---

2. The UK target has already been mentioned. Governor Schwarzenegger of California has proposed a target reduction for carbon dioxide of 80% by 2050.

example, land degradation and deforestation. Also targets must be realistic; the promotion of unachievable targets is counterproductive. Adequate analysis as to how targets are to be realized must be carried out before targets are proposed or publicized.

New paradigms

We need not only goals but also new attitudes and approaches in the drive towards sustainability – again at all levels of society, international, national and individual. Let me mention just two examples. First, we need to look seriously at measures of sustainability and accounting tools to apply those measures (see Arrow et al. 2004; Porritt 2005; also Chapter 6). The dominance of the 'market' is often also allowed to ride over environmental considerations. The economy, the market and the principles of free trade are 'tools' (important tools), but they must not be allowed to be in the position of 'masters'.

A second example of a new attitude to be taken on board, again at all levels from the international to the individual, is that of 'sharing'. At the individual level, a lot of sharing already occurs; at the international level it occurs much less. Perhaps the worst condemnation is that globally the rich are getting richer while the poor get poorer – the flow of wealth in the world is from the poor to the rich; the overwhelming balance of benefit is to rich nations rather than poor ones. Nations need to learn to share on a very much larger and more equitable scale.

We often talk of the 'global commons' meaning air, oceans and Antarctica – by definition these are 'commons' to be shared. But more 'commons' need to be included. For instance, there are respects in which fish and other marine stocks or land should be treated as resources to be shared. Or, in order for international action regarding climate change to be pursued, how are allowable emissions from fossil fuel burning or from deforestation to be allocated? How do we as a world share these natural resources, especially between the very rich, like ourselves, and the very poor? And how should we share our skills in science and technical 'know-how' with those who lack them?

One of the biggest 'sharing' challenges faced by the international community is how emissions of carbon dioxide can be shared fairly between nations. Great disparity exists between emissions by rich nations compared with poorer ones. Expressed in tonnes of carbon per capita per annum, they range from about 5.5 for the USA, 2.2 for Europe to 0.7 for China and 0.2 for India. The global average per capita is about 1 tonne per annum, and this must fall substantially during the twenty-first century. The FCCC will soon start negotiations regarding emissions allocations for all countries. One proposal is that the starting point should be current emissions, so that reduction levels from the present are negotiated. That is called 'grandfathering'. A proposal by the Global Commons Institute (www.gci.org.uk) is that emissions should first be allocated equally to everybody in the world per capita, then transfer of allocations should be allowed through trading between nations. The logic and basic equity of this proposal is in principle quite compelling , but is it achievable?

Sustainability will never be achieved without a great deal more sharing. Sharing is an important Christian principle. John the Baptist preached about sharing (Luke 3:11), Jesus talked about it (Luke 12:33), the early church were prepared to share everything (Acts 4:32) and Paul advocated the practice (2 Cor. 8:13–15). The opposite of sharing – greed and covetousness – is condemned throughout Scripture.

It is often more helpful to share skills (e.g. in science and technology) than material goods; this is being recognized more and more by aid agencies. I am a trustee of the Shell Foundation, a large charity set up by the Shell Company, particularly to support the provision of sustainable energy in poor countries. The Foundation's programmes are increasingly directed towards the creation and loan financing of enterprises. Examples of projects supported are the building and marketing of simple stoves that raise the efficiency of traditional fuels, reducing both the amount of fuel used and the health hazard from indoor air pollution; or that provide sustainable and affordable energy to poor communities from readily available waste material (e.g. rice straw in China, coconut shells in the Philippines). The potential for the spread of projects like these is enormous. One aim of the Foundation is to encourage the major scaling-up of such programmes so that they become significant both in the provision of energy to poor communities and in reducing greenhouse gas emissions.

Ways of sharing and of measuring our environmental impacts are needed for guidance to policy-makers, but they must also be espoused by the public at large. If not, government will not possess the confidence to act. For the public to take them on board, the public have to understand them. To understand, they have to be informed. There is a great need for accurate and understandable information to be propagated about all aspects of sustainability. Christian churches could play a significant role in this.

We, in the developed countries have already benefited over many generations from abundant fossil fuel energy. The demands on our stewardship take on a special poignancy as we realize that the adverse impacts of climate change will fall disproportionately on poorer nations and will tend to exacerbate the increasingly large divide between rich and poor.

My wife always reminds me when I speak on global problems that I need to indicate the sorts of actions individuals can take. There are some things all of us can do. For instance, when purchasing vehicles or appliances we can choose ones that are fuel efficient; we can ensure our homes are as energy efficient as possible; we can purchase our electricity from a 'green' supplier guaranteeing it is from renewable sources; we can use public transport, car-share more frequently, or travel less. Also we can support leaders in government or industry who are advocating or organizing the necessary solutions. To quote from Edmund Burke, a British parliamentarian from the eighteenth century, 'No one made a greater mistake than he who did nothing because he could do so little.'

In conclusion, I like very much the symbol of the Celtic Cross, the cross of Jesus surrounded by a circle denoting the world, illustrating that the redemption Jesus accomplished includes not only humankind but will also apply to the rest of creation after he returns to establish his kingdom on earth (Isa. 11:4–9; Rom. 8:19–23). We humans have the responsibility of being stewards of God's creation until Jesus returns. In a parable about stewardship in Luke 12, Jesus instructs his disciples and ends with the clear message 'Unto whomsoever much is given, of him shall much be required' (Authorized Version). The challenge to all of us is unmistakeable and daunting. But we also have the assurance that we do not have to act on our own. As God walked with Adam and Eve in the garden in the Genesis story, so he will come alongside us to help us as we seek to do his work here on earth.

© John Houghton, 2007

4. THOUGHTS ON THE SUSTAINABILITY OF THE NON-HUMAN WORLD

Ghillean T. Prance

Sir Ghillean Prance, FRS, VMH, committed himself to Christ in his first year at Oxford University. He was Director of the Royal Botanic Gardens 1988–99, and prior to that Vice-President for Science and Director of the Institute of Economic Botany at the New York Botanic Garden. He is now Scientific Director of the Eden Project in Cornwall and a visiting professor at Reading University; he is a past president of the Linnean Society and of the Institute of Biology, a trustee of both A Rocha and Au Sable and was President of Christians in Science (2003–6). Sir Ghillean is a Fellow of the Royal Society of London and a recipient of a host of honours, including the Victoria Medal of the Royal Horticultural Society. He has made many botanical expeditions to Amazonia and written widely on the ethics of conservation and the consequences of environmental mismanagement. He is the author of The Earth under Threat: A Christian Perspective (*Wild Goose Publications, 1996*); *his biography,* A Passion for Plants, *was written by Clive Langmead (Kew Publications, 2nd ed., 2001).*

Introduction

This book is about one of the most important issues facing environmentally conscious Christians, that of sustainability. The concept of sustainability has been seriously on the world agenda since the publication of the Brundtland Report (World Commission on Environment and Development, 1987). It was further boosted by wide-reaching environmental initiatives, especially by the Convention on Biological Diversity and the other achievements of the 1992 Earth Summit of Rio de Janeiro (such as the Framework Convention on Climate Change, the excellent Rio Declaration, and Agenda 21).

There have been various definitions of the concept of sustainability, but the underlying idea is that present human needs should not be at the expense of future generations. Perhaps we could learn from the woodland Indians of eastern North America who consider the effects of environmentally sensitive actions on the seventh unborn generation. However, a glance at the use of almost any non-human resource shows we are far from achieving this sort of attitude. Life in our society revolves around a four- or five-year term of political office rather than the long-term future. Moreover, the promotion of the sustainable use of any resource almost inevitably results in conflicts of interest between the promoter and those with a short-term interest to use up the resource and get rich quickly (see Chapter 6). In the process of unsustainable use, the few usually get rich at the expense of the poor. This involves explicit ethical and moral questions and is surely where our Christian faith must enter into the equation.

Dependence on the non-human world

In autumn 2005, the Eden Project in Cornwall opened a new educational building to demonstrate the services that plants and the environment provide for us and the other organisms with which we share this planet. It highlights plants at work in a closed environmental chamber, showing a life support system taken for granted by most people, where photosynthesis by plants provides the oxygen we breathe, the transpiration of plants influences our weather, and plants remove toxic substances from our air and water. But this system is our own life support system. The hope is that this exhibit will stimulate more respect and care for these unheralded, uncosted and essential services of the environment.

The living world provides us with much more than these basic services: we have learned how to use it for shelter, food, medicines, recreation, symbols of religion and too many other benefits to list here. We take all this for granted without counting the true cost of abuse and unsustainable use. Costanza et al. (1997) estimated that the total worldwide value of the natural processes is $33 trillion. They calculated this on the basis of the contributions from various ecosystems such as oceans, forests, grassland, wetlands, lakes and rivers, cropland; and of processes such as pollination of crops, climate regulation and biological pest control. At present we get the ecological systems that sustain the earth for free. But life on the planet will be unsustainable in the long term if we do not protect these services; at present we take them entirely for granted. We need to do something to account for these benefits in our environmental regulations and tax systems.

Destruction of our life support system

I began preparing this chapter as I was travelling down the river Amazon. The sky was hazy and the full glory of the sun was hidden for several days. It was the dry season and everyone was burning the areas of forest they had cut for their fields. Most of the current deforestation in Brazil is to grow soy beans, mainly for export to Europe to feed cattle and poultry. The Brazilian government's own statistics showed that the second largest area of forest loss ever recorded (23,500 sq km) occurred in 2004. Will this result in sustainable use of the areas that have been deforested? In many cases the answer is 'no', because of the poor soils of the region. Worse, the burning is sending large quantities of carbon dioxide and other gasses into the environment and hence contributing to climate change.

On the same trip on the Amazon I also saw large rafts of logs being floated down the river to the sawmills of Manaus. The species of trees with the best timber are being systematically – and illegally – eliminated from the forest without any thought of the future. For a short while some people are making a lot of money, but with no thought for their grandchildren.

It is unnecessary to travel to Brazil to encounter examples of unsustainable abuses of the environment. Look at what we have done to the stocks of cod and other fish in the North Sea and off the coast of Newfoundland. Another resource being quickly depleted and unsustainably used around the world is soil. The erosion and loss of soil is a major concern. Why would we fritter away the very substrate necessary to feed us? There is no need to list more examples of unsustainable practice, because at least today we are aware of this issue. What should be the Christian response to such poor stewardship of our planet?

Sustainability in a Christian context

Much traditional theology taught the superiority of humans over the rest of creation. We alone are created in the 'image of God', which is something no non-human part of creation can claim. Lynn White (1967) called Christianity 'the most anthropocentric religion the world has seen'. We must admit there is a lot of truth in this. However, White was not just criticizing our faith; he was also appealing for action through recommending Christians to regard St Francis as the patron saint of ecology. What seems to have been forgotten for a long time is the extensive biblical teaching about the non-human part of creation (Berry 2003) and about justice for all people. In this age of unsustainable and unprecedented environmental destruction, this is where our theology should be placing more emphasis.

For example, 'And the LORD God made all kinds of trees grow out of the ground – trees that were pleasing to the eye and good for food' (Gen. 2:9). The trees are for enjoyment and not just to use to extinction. Genesis places the aesthetic before the utilitarian.

We find a complete integrated ecology of the ecosystem in the words of the psalmist:

> The trees of the LORD are well watered,
>   the cedars of Lebanon that he planted,
> There the birds make their nests;
>   the stork has its home in the pine trees.
> The high mountains belong to the wild goats;
>   the crags are a refuge for the conies.
> (Ps. 104:16–18)

Many other passages also show that creation brings pleasure to God and should also to the people he created in his own image.

Care of creation

> For six years you are to sow your fields and harvest the crops, but during the seventh year let the land lie unploughed and unused. Then the poor among your people may get food from it, and the wild animals may eat what they leave. Do the same with your vineyard and your olive grove.
>
> — Exodus 23:10–11

It is significant that these verses about the sabbath of the land take into account both the poor and the beasts of the field. One of the most serious environmental problems we are facing today is soil erosion. It has been calculated we are losing about seventy-five billion tonnes of topsoil a year by wind and water erosion, mostly from agricultural land (Pimentel et al. 1995). Allowing the land to rest and recuperate permits it to be used sustainably. Many of the indigenous peoples with whom I have worked allow the soil to rest from time to time and plant species that reduce erosion.

Justice

> If anyone has material possessions and sees his brother in need but has no pity on him, how can the love of God be in him?
>
> — 1 John 3:17

This is just one of many biblical verses that appeals to us to be concerned for fellow human beings less fortunate than us. For a long time the Western church has not listened properly to the part of God's Word that bids us to respect and care for creation and fellow humans. Instead, we have been ready to accept the unsustainable pathway of the rest of the world led by extravagant lifestyles, greed and the financial institutions, and this at the expense of the poor. This fact really struck me midway through my career as I began to witness the increased pace of destruction of the Amazon rainforest. This greedy exploitation has made a few people rich but made many more people poorer. I began my scientific career as a plant taxonomist and ecologist interested in forest biology. In the mid-1970s it became apparent that forests were being rapidly destroyed for mainly short-term gains, such as cattle pasture. In response to this, and partially motivated by a growing interest in creation theology and care, I began to place much more research emphasis on practical issues, through concentrating on ethnobotany and economic botany aimed at sustainable use of the environment. In some ways this is when my Christian faith and my scientific work came together.

Some examples of sustainable practice

Non-timber forest products
One way of using the forest without destroying it is through the marketing of non-timber forest products (NTFPs) that can be extracted without cutting down the trees. There is an extensive literature on this (see Ros-Tonen, Dijkman & Van Bueren 1995; Prance 1998). I have done taxonomic and ecological research on one of the best of all these non-timber forest products, the Brazil nut (*Bertholletia excelsa*). The research we did on the pollination of this species showed it needs to be grown in or near forests where the pollinators are available, rather than in isolated plantations. Brazil nuts are still nearly all gathered from the forest floor, not by replacing the native forest with plantations. In Brazil the governments of some states have set up extractivist reserves where the local people are allowed to extract NTFPs from the forest, but not

to cut down the trees themselves. These reserves are having some success in encouraging the sustainable use of the forest, but provide only a meagre living for the inhabitants. The challenge is to develop more NTFPs and to find ways in which value can be added to them.

An example of how this may be done is Amazon-Coop, a project in the town of Altamira in the Pará State of Brazil. Here the local people and Indians harvest Brazil nuts from the forest, but also run a small factory to extract the oil for the nuts. This adds value to the product, which is then sold directly to the Body Shop for use in their cosmetics. Adding value in this way makes NTFPs more sustainable, because it is more viable economically. The direct purchase of a forest product from the producers means they get a fair deal without going through a long chain of intermediaries. In the case of Amazon-Coop this is done as a cooperative, so all individuals involved are owners of the enterprise and get a fair share of the profit. The fair trade in Brazil nuts and other non-timber products from the Amazon can help to promote sustainable use of the forest. Even timber can be extracted sustainably where there is a will. At present in most places in the tropics timber is a resource mined through overexploitation rather than managed. It is important for us to promote 'fair trade' products.

Plants of the north-east

One of the largest projects I helped to set up while Director of the Royal Botanic Gardens was called Plantas do Nordeste (Plants of the North-East [PNE]). The purpose of the programme was to find sustainable uses for the plants in the arid north-east region of Brazil. Its slogan was 'Local plants for local people'. PNE had three parts:

- *A survey of the regional biodiversity*: since the first problem was the identification of plants and of vegetation types, the biodiversity component was an essential first step, carried out in collaboration with local universities.
- *An economic botany component*: to find ways to use the plants for sustainable income in a poverty-stricken region. It included

such topics as plants for goat fodder to manage goats in corrals rather than letting them free to harm vegetation; plants for honey production from native bees; plants to make inexpensive medicines for the poor; and plants for the production of dried flowers.

- *An informatics component:* to make available all the information gathered by the other two parts, carried out in cooperation with the computer department of a university in Recife.

The programme brought together many local universities and institutions, both governmental and non-governmental. In a small way it is contributing to a better utilization of the plant resources of the poorest region of Brazil.

Ecotourism

A way to help natural environments pay for themselves is through ecotourism. I have been involved in this in several places. As I wrote the first draft of this chapter, I was cruising down the Amazon with a group of British tourists. It was a local river boat constructed in a small Amazon town up the Rio Negro. The crew and guides were all local people. Along the rivers we bought fish to eat and other local products. Such practices ensure that most of the money helps people of the region and not a foreign tour agency. Visitors get a firsthand experience of the Amazon ecosystem and much information about its use and abuse. From these tours I have interested a number of donors in supporting conservation in many different ways.

I also chair the Global Biodiversity Foundation, much of whose income to support work in ethnobotany and nutrition for local people comes from an ecotourism programme in Morocco. The foundation provides for ecological and ethnobotanical projects in Morocco, Malaysia and Mexico from tourist income. Unfortunately, there are many projects advertised as ecotourism that really lack the 'eco'. It is important to make sure that any ecotourism project does no harm to the local ecosystem and also benefits the local people. It requires the involvement of responsible and knowledgeable scientists.

Conservation

One of the most important parts of achieving a sustainable world is the conservation of the great diversity of species and habitats in the world. It is witnessed by the much-quoted title of a book I co-authored in 1967, *Extinction Is Forever* (Prance & Elias 1976). Involvement in conservation has been an important part of my own scientific work for many years. I have used my taxonomic data to identify centres of endemism and priority areas for conservation. At present I have a three-year Darwin Initiative grant for work in the Yaboti Biosphere Reserve in Misiones, Argentina, involving both ethnobotanical work with the local Guaraní population and the preparation of a management plan for the reserve. I also chair the Brazilian Atlantic Rainforest Trust that has set up a reserve in the much-depleted Mata Atlantica of coastal Brazil. Funds have gradually been raised in the UK for purchase of land now run as a reserve by a Brazilian non-governmental organization. The reserve is also partially supported by ecotourism that uses a nicely restored farmhouse for accommodation.

The Eden Project

I am the Scientific Director of the Eden Project in Cornwall. This enterprise has been a huge success as a visitor attraction, not least because from the start it set out with a clearly defined mission: to show the vital importance of plants to people and to promote their sustainable use. All we do in interpretation to visitors to the Eden Project and in our scientific research programme there is geared towards these two goals. Behind the scenes, the project has a waste neutral policy now achieving through extensive recycling a food waste digester, composting and the purchase of recycled products wherever possible. These are all reasons why I have been so delighted to be involved with a project that has so successfully hijacked a biblical name!

Conclusion

The twin motives of my Christian faith and my concern for the environment have deeply influenced the emphasis of my more recent research projects; the key issue has been to promote the sustainable stewardship of creation. In order to achieve a sustainable society, new approaches and new attitudes requiring a moral and ethical stance will be required. This is where religion must play an important part. There is much about creation care in the Bible, and we are not being good stewards unless we heed this and respect the whole of creation. It was made to be enjoyed and not destroyed: 'God saw all that he had made, and it was very good' (Gen. 1:31). Unfortunately, it is no longer so good because of what man has done to it. I have given examples here from the distant Amazon, where I have been involved, but there is also much to do closer to home. Creation care is not an optional activity for the Christian; it is an obligation, for we must care for the poor and the beasts of the earth, as Exodus 23:10–11 instructs us to do.

© Ghillean T. Prance, 2007

5. CONSUMPTION AND HAPPINESS: CHRISTIAN VALUES AND AN APPROACH TOWARDS SUSTAINABILITY

Brian Heap and Flavio Comim

Professor Sir Brian Heap, CBE, ScD, FRS, is a Research Associate at the Capability and Sustainability Centre, St Edmund's College, Cambridge, and edits Philosophical Transactions of the Royal Society (Biological Sciences). *Formerly, he was Master of St Edmund's College, and Vice-President and Foreign Secretary of the Royal Society.*

Flavio Comim, PhD, is an economist and Director of the Capability and Sustainability Centre, St Edmund's College. He was a Lead Coordinating Author of the Millennium Assessment Project. He is supported by Trinity College, Cambridge, the United Nations Environment Programme and the International Labour Organization.

Our starting point is a belief that sustainable consumption and production practices are fundamental to the future success and planetary survival of humankind and that these practices have been informed by Judeo-Christian teaching about stewardship and responsibility. The converse of this is that the problems with unsustainable patterns of consumption and production include a negative impact on individuals' well-being and happiness. This leads us to ask what a blueprint based on the Christian value system might look like for a repair of the created order, and what contribution would be expected of us as 'reasoned agents' of change rather than 'needy patients'. We focus on life in more developed countries because this is where the greatest challenges of overconsumption and profligacy exist, topics we too often prefer to sideline. We suggest that Christian values provide powerful and timely insights into stewardship responsibility, the integrity of creation, exploitation through self-interest and greed, love for our neighbours and care for the needs of future generations. This is not to diminish the importance of the challenges in less developed countries, nor to ignore the significance of a comprehensive global ethic, but these are topics that have been analysed extensively elsewhere.

Introduction

Consumption has increased immensely over the second half of the twentieth century, a period over which overall economic activity has quintupled, energy use more than quadrupled, food production tripled, and world population more than doubled. Business-as-usual scenarios suggest a slowing of these trends rates until 2055, though consumption rates are predicted to increase at well beyond the rate of population growth, and energy is anticipated to show a fivefold increase over the next hundred years (Heap & Kent 2000; Heap 2003, 2004).

Nowadays, more than 25% of individuals worldwide live a lifestyle once limited to rich nations. This laudable improvement means that, while the average Chinese and Indian still consumes much less than the average North American or European, their combined consumer class is larger than that of all western Europe. In China, 240 million people have been classified as 'new consumers' and there will soon be more of them than the total number of consumers in the USA. At least one-fifth of global car ownership is attributable to these 'new consumers' and by 2010 this figure could have risen to one-third (Myers & Kent 2004). The explosive rise of living standards in China is reflected by a 2.5-fold increase since 1994 in household incomes, the ownership of colour televisions (82% of households now own one), landline phones (63%), video players (52%) and mobile phones (at least one phone in roughly 400m households).

Despite this, the proportion of Chinese expressing satisfaction with the way things are in their lives has actually declined over time, mostly because of the ills associated with the urban environment compared with the lifestyle of their rural counterparts (Gallup 2005) – a telling example that consumption and economic prosperity have not delivered a 'promised land' for its inhabitants. How does this relate to the conventional sustainability paradigm necessary for long-term global survival and functioning, and how does it fit with the cherished values foundational to Christian principles and attitudes (see the table below)?

Formulating a Christian framework directed towards sustainability calls to mind an important medieval distinction recalled by the economist and Nobel laureate Amartya Sen, who argues that the focus in such a debate should be placed not only on people as human beings whose needs deserve attention as 'needy patients', but also on their role as 'reasoned agents' whose freedom to determine what we should safeguard and sustain can extend far beyond our living standards and needs (Sen 2003: 14). The sustainability approach should celebrate and try to safeguard human freedoms, says Sen, much as the apostle Paul insisted in his letter to the

Table: Christian principles ansd values that map on to sustainability

Christian message	Sustainability approach
Stewardship responsibility	Concern with environmental degradation
Integrity and renewal of creation	Dematerialization and informed consumption and production
Loving my neighbour and the common good	Deliberative democracy and participatory public debate
Concern for future generations	Intergenerational criteria of global equality
Criticism of self-interest, greed and exploitation	Equitable distribution of wealth between less and more developed countries

Galatians, 'It is for freedom that Christ has set us free. Stand firm, then, and do not let yourselves be burdened again by a yoke of slavery' (Gal. 5:1).

Those who first encounter the idea of sustainable consumption and production are often worried that it will require the introduction of draconian rules and regulations, but sacrifices in living standards may not actually be substantial – in fact, quite possibly, just the contrary (Sen 2003: 6). Our argument is that sustainable consumption and production practices are fundamental to the planetary survival of humankind, never mind its continuing success, and that these practices derive their substance from Christian messages and values about stewardship and responsibility. We concentrate here on life in more developed countries, since they face the immediate challenges of unsustainable consumption and production, while in less developed countries the reality is more often underconsumption and low production. This is not to minimize the importance of the problem in less developed countries nor to deny the wholesome significance of a global ethic (such as that developed by the Parliament of the World's Religions in 1993, which encompasses parallel contributions of other world faiths; Küng 1996). Rather, it is our intention to focus on the Christian message because it has not always received the attention it deserves in this area.

What drives consumption?

Advocating a conscious move towards sustainable consumption and production requires a multidimensional and multidisciplinary analysis if a strategy that speaks to the wider community (including policy-makers) is to have an effect.

Population growth is frequently perceived as a macrodriver of consumption and unsustainability, but the picture is not as straightforward as sometimes suggested. Britain has a population growth of 0.1%, adding an extra 59,000 people each year to a population of 60 million. Bangladesh has a growth rate of 2.2%, producing an extra 3.2 million people per year to go with 147 million. Each new British consumer uses 45 times more fossil fuel than each new Bangladeshi, so that the population growth in this country produces almost as much carbon dioxide emission as the 54 times larger population growth of Bangladesh. In countries such as China, India, Brazil, Mexico and Russia the combination of population growth and economic development is resulting in a class of new consumers likely to redraw the economic map of the world. By 2010 it is estimated that new consumers alone in these countries could well number over a billion and account for 20% of the world's purchasing power (Myers & Kent 2004).

The urge to acquire must have been one of the innate drives that enabled the survival of our earliest ancestors. It differs today only to the extent that rational analysis plays a part in our choices. The dominant view of human behaviour emerging from studies in evolutionary adaptation and psychology is that the adoption of a sustainable lifestyle is countercultural and will not come naturally. Such a lifestyle presents a special challenge because it is insatiable as well as immediate and inbuilt. We get little help from our genes because they are selfish and, in the words of Dawkins (2001), have made us what we are.

Centuries earlier, the apostle Paul wrestled with the same problem and came to a different conclusion. While Paul understood that to change selfish behaviour was a tough assignment, he recognized that fundamental change was possible. The flash of revelation that life could be lived differently came in his case from the recently crucified Jesus Christ, whose life, death, resurrection and teaching transformed not only the direction of Paul's life and value system but that of others of his generation and beyond. Nonetheless, the challenge of selfish genes was never far away – 'I do not understand what I do. For what I want to do I do not do, but what I hate I do' (Rom. 7:15).

Consumer behavioural traits may offer selective advantages but at the same time be pathological and irrational. Psychological denial may manifest as a failure to face up to health-threatening behaviour, as in obese consumers, but even to an impending potential disaster. Pollsters assessing people's attitude about the possibility of a dam bursting high above where they lived found that concern fell to zero the nearer you approached the dam (Diamond 2005). In the present context, any proposal for change concerning consumption and production must contend with self-serving behaviour and denial, but must also appeal to the importance of strengthening collectively those social and moral behaviours that influence consumption patterns and value the planet for both our own future happiness and that of future generations. In other words, we need to distinguish between a singular view of consumption and production that reflects individualistic trends and selfish behaviour, and a normative position that addresses how we should behave for social and moral forms of consumption and production that enhance well-being.

Pursuit of happiness

For most people, happiness is the main, if not the only, ultimate objective of life (Ng 1996). However, there are two senses in which happiness can represent a state of people's well-being. The traditional sense is of happiness as a one-dimensional hedonic expression of our feelings. It conveys the message that happiness is a transitory and subtle representation of our self-satisfaction with life. The second sense is about happiness as an expression of a fulfilling life. Its message is that happiness is achieved through our long-term goals and sense of autonomy in our daily affairs of life.

Attempts to measure what gives us greatest happiness are not easy (Nettle 2005). Subjective happiness expressed in pleasant affects such as elation, joy, contentment and ecstasy has been assessed by physiological and neurobiological indicators, by observing social and non-verbal behaviour and by questionnaires. In order of importance, the five most important factors are family relationships, financial situation, work, community and friends, and health. Personal freedom and personal values also play a major part (see Layard 2005); it is claimed that happiness can be lastingly increased (Seligman 2002).

Individual perception of standard of living is regularly mentioned as one of the most important elements of happiness. Annual surveys of more than twenty thousand students entering colleges in the USA show a growing proportion asserting it was very important to be rich and a declining number saying it was very important to develop a meaningful philosophy in life (see Myers 2002). Nonetheless, the correlation in the USA between happiness and income is only 0.2 (National Opinion Research Centre, quoted in Easterlin 2000), while in Switzerland the highest-income recipients report a lower sense of well-being than the income group immediately below (Frey & Stutzer 2002). Clearly, there are many reasons why high income and material prosperity do not simply translate into greater happiness. Aggregated indicators of material well-being say very little about how higher income levels are distributed among different individuals and social groups. It is logically possible that income per capita grows with higher income concentration: people compare themselves with others and their relative income is what becomes important. Moreover, aspiration levels adjust to the rise in income (the 'hedonic treadmill effect'); people get used to the higher income level, which then produces less happiness for them than they would enjoy if no such adjustment had taken place. Lottery winners are very happy after winning, but their happiness levels revert near to the original level after some weeks. The clear conclusion from happiness research is that the relationship between happiness and per capita income is not close, though it is well established that people in rich countries are generally happier than those in poor countries (Frey & Stutzer 2002).

Many good reasons exist why Christians should be happy and why we should enjoy our faith in God through Jesus Christ. We praise God not primarily out of duty but out of enjoyment. There is evidence that people who believe in God are happier because they experience the discovery of the deepest and most enduring happiness in God, a happiness that reaches its fulfilment when it is shared with others through its loving expression (Myers 1992). It is a natural part of worship, praise and virtue, and is implicit in Paul's letters to Christians in Corinth and Rome ('whether you eat or drink or whatever you do, do it all for the glory of God' [1 Cor. 10:31]; 'for from him and through him and to him are all things. / To him be the glory for ever!' [Rom. 11:36]). Moreover, Christian teaching helps us to understand the grounds of faith: what we believe about God, what God has done to save and win us for himself, how to distinguish between truth and falsehood, the nature of our new value system, and the rules and guidelines for daily living (Col. 3:1–10); all these give a security that underlies and reinforces our happiness. Furthermore, we should be happy because of faith in the future.

Christians who live in the relatively prosperous First World have to live out their faith in the face of conspicuous profligacy and abuse of the planet's resources. As Christians and consumers we are free to pursue our lifestyle through a rational choice model, or to become locked into what Jackson (2005) calls a 'social pathology' driven by social norms and advertising. If happiness is the main, if not the only, ultimate objective of life for most individuals, the question becomes whether our society has become seriously adrift because we simultaneously degrade our own psychological and social well-being through consumer-driven acquisition of economic goods accompanied by damage to natural capital (Jackson 2005).

Summarizing so far: consumption, although necessary for human welfare, is not a sufficient requirement for happiness, while prosperity gained at the expense of the habitability of the planet is perverse. If unsustainable consumption has such a low impact on individuals' well-being, is there an alternative based on Christian values?

Towards a Christian famework

The Bible speaks of how God intends us to live and how we should construct and reconstruct the world and our lifestyles – in peace and harmony, in social justice, in humility and in faith. Although the churches today regard cultivating a religious sense of humility and awe towards the natural world as one of their prime tasks, a Report of Churches Together in Britain and Ireland (2005) argued that in the past the churches sanctioned an exploitative culture and that this has to be recognized and replaced for the common good if the planet is to be saved for future generations – our culture must change to underpin the far-reaching changes in lifestyle and culture urgently needed. The covenant Yahweh made with the people of Israel after Adam and Eve were expelled from the fruitful and peaceable Garden of Eden promised a land 'flowing with milk and honey' (Exod. 3:8), close to paradise. Murray (1992) calls it a 'cosmic covenant': it encompassed both the land and all its inhabitants within its embrace; it spoke of God's rescue of all creation and not just humankind.

Yet self-interest, greed and exploitation asserted themselves as the Israelites became settled in the land and followed other gods: the rich appropriated the wealth of the land for themselves, the just laws of good governance were abandoned, and the poor and downtrodden were sidelined. The land suffered and environmental degradation set in, which affected the inhabitants of the earth (Isa. 5:8–10; 24:1–6); Abraham and his nephew, Lot, were forced to go their separate ways because the land could not support them and their families if they stayed together (Gen. 5:6); and in due course few men were left (Hab. 3:17). Many other biblical passages reveal the distorting connections between human injustice and the distribution of wealth, and environmental exploitation and degradation of the created order (Northcott 2001).

As Pope Benedict XVI said in his inaugural address, failure to address the demands of sustainability threatens the created order, 'the external deserts in the world are growing, because the internal deserts have become so vast. Therefore the earth's treasures no longer serve to build God's garden for all to live in, but they have been made to serve the powers of exploitation and destruction' (Benedict XVI 2005). Incontrovertible proofs of social injustice are everywhere: inefficient production and overconsumption of resources in more developed countries; deprivation and degradation of communities due to underconsumption, together with the impact of hazardous waste from industrialized countries in less developed countries. Two examples testify to the alarming impact of our unsustainable practices on our distant neighbours: the millions of tons of waste transported each year, such as redundant electronic goods to China; and industrial residues detected in people living in remote areas of the world, such as East Greenland and Siberia (Diamond 2005). Such disregard for intergenerational justice is tantamount to theft in the same way as the thief who came to steal, kill and destroy the sheep (John 10:10), an illustration

Jesus used to emphasize that his mission is both to bring freedom and make it fully available.

Any Christian framework of sustainable consumption therefore demands at its source the recognition of God as creator and redeemer, revealed through the life, death and resurrection of Jesus Christ. As Paul wrote, '[God] made known to us the mystery of his will according to his good pleasure, which he purposed in Christ, to be put into effect when the times will have reached their fulfilment – to bring all things in heaven and on earth together under one head, even Christ' (Eph. 1:9–10). For the early Christians, understanding Christ as Redeemer was a challenging insight not only into his saving relationship to humanity but also his redemption of the whole created order and his countering of the expression of sin and evil in all their forms (Northcott 2001). Paul spoke dramatically of the whole creation groaning because it was caught in a downward spiral of decay 'right up to the present time' and was awaiting release (Rom. 8:22). None of this is an excuse for thinking that action can be delayed, but rather that we should possess a deep passion for right thinking, justice and care of the created order. We cannot escape the question 'What does the LORD require of you?' The answer Micah gives is that we should do justice and love mercy, and walk humbly with our God (Mic. 6:8), a fitting reminder that 'justice is something to be done, something that is inherently relational or social' (Forrester 2001: 198).

Contents of a blueprint

Can we devise a blueprint for sustainable consumption and production that embraces both our divinely ordained role of Christian stewardship and our common desire for true happiness? It must be multidimensional and engage Christians of all traditions and disciplines. Henry Ford created a mental picture of large numbers of people buying and driving a low-priced dream car long before it was ever committed to paper. The idea gradually matured and eventually became a reality. A blueprint for sustainable consumption and production must offer a distinct approach, while incoporating the familiar themes of stewardship, responsibility, choices, injustices and intergenerational elements. It will have to engage with the decline of religious belief and social solidarity in the last century and the rise in individualism and progress of science, factors that have left us with two dominant ideas in more developed countries: Darwin's theory of evolution from which many have drawn the conclusion that you have to be selfish to survive; and the perception (incorrectly) attributed to Adam Smith of an 'invisible hand', where if everyone is completely selfish things will actually turn out for the best – free contracts between independent agents will produce the greatest possible happiness (Layard 2005: 231).

The modern dilemma is that the desire for happiness is not guaranteed by an obsession with economic growth and unbridled consumption. This provides an opportunity to consider a more hopeful alternative. As long ago as 1795 the French mathematician and Enlightenment thinker Condorcet expressed the hope that people might reason their way into achieving technical progress as well as behavioural adjustments. He wrote that 'a very small amount of ground will be able to produce a great quantity of supplies of greater utility or higher quality; more goods will be obtained from a smaller outlay; the manufacture of articles will be achieved with less wastage in raw materials and will make better use of them' (cited in Sen 2003: 12). Condorcet had the prescience to anticipate the importance of sustainable consumption and production in a century when life was very different. However, neither Condorcet nor Malthus (1798) foresaw the remarkable impact of scientific and technological advances that would arrest the occurrence of widespread global famine.

Definitions and objectives
Sustainable consumption lies at the heart of the concept of sustainable development. It enriches our understanding of sustainable development because it emphasizes the need for consumption habits and attitudes to change (Arrow, Sen & Suzumura 1997; Sen 2004). The need for change was highlighted by the USA National Research Council (1999: 4), which concluded that 'many human needs will not be met, life support systems will be dangerously

degraded, and the number of hungry and poor will increase' unless there is a reversal of present trends of consumption, production and environmental neglect. Any attempt to define a strategy for change must include a recognition of *decisions, influenced by ethical demands, promoting better quality of life and environmental sustainability.* The practical objectives of sustainable consumption and production are broad:

- to reduce the consumption of natural resources by improvements in the efficiency of processes and services;
- to minimize the emissions of waste, pollutants and toxic materials over the life cycle of products, processes and services;
- to create new materials with long life, durability, and with re-use properties;
- to conserve biodiversity for current needs and freedoms; and
- to address disparities between more and less developed countries and protect the needs of future generations.

The extent of these objectives means that a compromise is almost unavoidable between the technological and the ethical dimensions of economic decisions if a definition of sustainable consumption and production is to carry enough consensus for practical purposes.

The challenges of sustainable consumption and production can be examined under at least five headings that address at the same time both how to consume differently while reducing our effect on the environment, a so-called 'double dividend' (Jackson 2005).

Science, engineering and technology
Certain advances in science and technology have already steered us almost inadvertently towards sustainable consumption and production. Some of these have been more influential than others. 'Dematerialization' has been a pervasive theme because it implies greater efficiencies in use, production and process. Numerous sectors (chemicals, pulp and paper, textiles, food, energy, metals and minerals) of production industries have used 'green chemistry' to reduce energy and water use and decrease waste output. Today's refrigerator-freezers in the UK consume an average of

50% less energy than those sold in 1997. The construction industry has built competitively priced houses in London with electricity initially derived from a combined heat and power unit using wood taken from sustainable tree management in local streets and parks: shared cars, low-allergy building materials to minimize respiratory problems of residents, and recycling techniques to reduce waste by 80%. The aim is to become carbon neutral with a reduced carbon dioxide footprint, now down by about 50% and a long-term objective of a 'zero-squared' project consisting of zero waste and zero carbon emissions.

What is more, the ingenuity of engineers in making and distributing useful consumer artefacts has resulted in an S-shaped pattern of growth in resource consumption during the last century: a lag period followed by exponential growth and then a plateau so that fewer materials are now used for a unit of production. Within the EU, motor manufacturers have been required to recycle 85% of a vehicle's weight by 2005; this will rise to 95% by 2015. In food production, advances in plant breeding have resulted in new hybrid rice for Africa that has 50% more grain than current varieties when cultivated without chemical fertilizers in traditional rain-fed systems. Genetically modified crops also reduce the chemical burden on the environment and people are exposed to lower levels of pesticides; such crops also diminish waste and pollution.

On the negative side, the Millennium Ecosystem Assessment (MA 2005) makes for sober reading, with some 60% of the planet's ecosystem services already degraded by human activities through atmospheric pollution from excess greenhouse gases, draining of freshwater aquifers, overharvesting of forests and fisheries, contamination of oceans and introduction of alien species to new regions. The world's coral reefs have diminished by 20%, and 40% of the planet's rivers have fragmented. Science and technology are faced with the mounting challenge of reversing the impact of unsustainable consumption. The work of the MA has been important in identifying the extent of global damage; advances are now being made in establishing the minimum viable populations for sustainability and in identifying indicators to monitor progress or decline.

Freedom exists in this sector to choose initiatives to mitigate the impacts of unsustainable consumption and production and thus any negative effects of population growth in less developed countries. This freedom will not be sufficient in itself to overcome unsustainability, because the crucial aspects of any solution will be consumers' behaviour and lifestyles together with the response of businesses and industry. Much work is needed to quantify the relative importance of technological 'fixes' and the adaptation of humans to environmental decay.

Consumption behaviour and lifestyle

Everyone has an individual right to prosper, yet at the same time every person has to recognize that others have the same right, wherever they are. This recognition has vast significance. The Christian church has a commitment to identify and oppose injustice and oppression, to stand alongside the marginalized and excluded, and to protect both present and future legitimate interests. Economic activity that leads to wealth creation is a major engine of greater well-being and we should celebrate it. However, the pursuit of profit as an end in itself frequently results in hardship, injustice and instability (Churches Together in Britain and Ireland 2005) because the conditions under which profit is pursued can lead to more income inequality.

People's lifestyle and consumption patterns are known to be affected by their conscious decisions about the future. Hamilton (2003a) argues that in a postmodern growth society much greater attention should be devoted to the way people think about their lives and relationships. He rejects ideologies and social structures driven by a fetish for growth. During the 1990s, 25% of British adults aged 30–59 chose to downshift in their lifestyles (rising to 30%, if those stopping work to look after a baby or set up their own businesses are included), not for the purpose of living closer to nature but because the excessive pursuit of money and materialism came at a substantial cost to people's lives and those of their families. Downshifting was slightly more common among women than men, but it was spread evenly across age groups and social grades. The average reduction in income was 40% (Hamilton 2003b).

Mathematical modelling helps to evaluate the complexities of such decision-making. One example from Japan shows that if households decreased cooking at home by 10% and increased eating at restaurants correspondingly, the demand for eating and drinking places would go up 1.49 times. This would increase total carbon dioxide emission by 0.3% (less sustainable) while landfill (waste) would decrease by 0.3% (more sustainable). However, the effect of spending more time and money at restaurants would mean that less was available to spend on other forms of consumption. If this 'rebound effect' is taken into account, it would lead to a significant reduction in emissions and waste, and the lifestyle would become more environmentally friendly (Takase, Kondo & Washizu 2005). If sustainable consumption and production is to be taken seriously by consumers and policy-makers, other examples need to be examined to help us construct an evidence-based argument (Hertwich 2005).

Industrial and business practices
When economic activity raises the standard of living of the population and relieves the distress of the poor, it can be seen as a component of God's will for the common good. In this sense the creation of wealth by economic activity is an important engine of greater well-being in the modern age, provided it is coupled to suitable distribution of the wealth and brings benefit to the disadvantaged (including less developed countries). It has the potential of producing a sufficiency of wealth in communities, pleasure and happiness, civilization and culture, and longevity with good health. If business conducts itself without a moral compass, it depletes the moral capital of the community; consequently, most cooperatives in the private sector are keen to project themselves as good corporate citizens. Small acts of selfishness, neglect or moral blindness in the industrial and business communities can be disproportionately damaging through the leverage of economic mechanisms and lead to great and continuing harm (Churches Together in Britain and Ireland 2005).

Business ethics and corporate social responsibility have become part of good management training and practice, and many believe that transformation of the relationship between business and living systems will dominate the twenty-first century (Hawken, Lovins & Lovins 2000; McDonough & Braungart 2002). There is still some way to go before this idea becomes universal, but market campaign activity has motivated change. Staples, the number one retailer of paper and office supplies in the USA, with annual sales of $11 billion per year, has agreed to stop selling products made from endangered forests and work towards a minimum average of 30% postconsumer recycled content in the paper products it sells. Nike, number one merchandiser of sports shoes in the world, with over $10 billion in annual sales, has been targeted by a group including Oxfam, Community Aid Abroad, Hong Kong Christian Industrial Committee and United Students Against Sweatshops and has agreed to phase out toxic products within ten years through green design. It is now the number one user of organic cotton for use in its garments, though it has still not agreed to pay a living wage to its workers. Dell is the largest seller of personal computers in the world, selling over $32 billion of electronic products per annum. The Computer-Take-Back Campaign has forced the recycling of PCs and raised awareness of the e-waste problem (O'Rourke 2005).

Transparency and accountability feature highly among the public priorities of today's industrial and business organizations. Industrial practices underwent a remarkable change in this respect when it was discovered that chlorofluorocarbon (CFC) compounds can have dramatic effects in the stratosphere. CFCs evaporate and recondense at room temperatures, but in the stratosphere they cause immense damage to the ozone layer and threaten human health (Rowland & Molina 1994). Political will was galvanized on an international scale to ban these products, though it took about twenty-six years from scientific discovery to full implementation of the ban (Brenton 1994). Molina, who shared a Nobel Prize in 1995, said that when the United States prohibited the use of CFCs as propellants in spray cans, experts believed the ban would put a lot of people out of work. It did not, because effective alternatives were found. Nonetheless, it will take more than a century for the chlorine to disappear from the stratosphere (Meadows et al. 1992). This example reminds us that consumers, and not just governments, have the ultimate responsibility both for their own behaviour and even for that of big businesses, because businesses change when the public come to expect and demand different behaviour, or otherwise make things difficult for them.

Fiscal measures

Consumption is widely perceived as an expression of a prosperous society. It helps to win votes at election time. Whether consumption can be taken to be good for us is another matter. We may see it as synonymous with improved well-being so that the more we consume the better off we are; or we may regard it as environmentally and psychologically threatening to our quality of life (Jackson 2005). Arguments for any change in attitude will have to be accessible as well as persuasive; this is where it becomes important to know where the responsibility lies and what may be done about it by parents and professional teachers (who have a fundamental role to ensure that the spiritual dimension is not ignored), the media (and the tone they set), the legal system and the churches (Churches Together in Britain and Ireland 2005).

Traditional economic measures such as the gross national product (GNP) used by the UK Treasury also lead to flawed decisions. GNP is deeply engrained in political life as an assessment of a nation's economic progress and standing. However, a nation's capital assets can take several forms; they require measures of the net changes in manufactured and human capital, public knowledge and natural capital. As an indicator, GDP is insensitive to the depreciation of capital assets and does not recognize the net value of changes in externalities such as the environment-resource base (Arrow et al. 2004). As a result, consumers are confused about true costs. If wealth and social well-being are taken as equivalent, it is possible that GNP can increase for a time, even while the country becomes poorer and social well-being declines. Dasgupta (2001: 149) is unequivocal: 'the moral is banal: GNP is not a measure of the quality of life'. If we were to get used to the term 'net national product' (NNP), which has been proposed as an alternative, it would represent a more realistic assessment of sustainable development by taking account of and internalizing environmental costs (Dasgupta 1998, 2001).

Another measure of well-being is the United Nations Development Index, though neither this nor NNP are related to wealth (Dasgupta 2001). A different approach has been developed in the USA, where Daly and Cobb (1989) have developed an Index of Sustainable Economic Welfare (ISEW). This index adjusts the GNP, a personal-consumption-based measure, to account for a variety of social and environmental factors not generally included in measuring economic progress. The Yale Center for Environmental Law and Policy team has designed an Environmental Sustainability Index (2005) for individual countries that measures their overall progress towards sustainability to provide and protect the environment for future generations. Others prefer measures such as the ecological rucksack (denoting the real burden carried by a product, including costs invisible to the consumer), the ecological footprint (providing an equivalent value of land usage) or the environment space (reflecting the freedom required to enable people to live in a certain way). The conclusion from all these studies is that no country can be said to be on a sustainable environmental path, and that improved and transparent evaluations for each country envisaged by the ESI would focus attention on the environmental costs of modern lifestyles.

Policies designed for sustainable consumption and production must demonstrate the true costs of modern lifestyles, their environmental impact and the success or otherwise of fiscal measures such as subsidies. It is uncomfortable reading for most of us when we visit a website that provides entry into one's personal ecological footprint (http://www.bestfootforward.com) and gives a visual gateway of the impact of our unsustainable consumption lifestyles. It is even worse if we consider that one of the chief roles of a Christian is to be a co-worker with God in the continuous repair of the created order (which has the tendency to decay into disorganized systems), to bring new things into existence and to establish new patterns of order (Rom. 8:20). God's original creative work made order out of chaos, and our calling is to make more order yet, co-operating with God's creativity as human beings made in the image of God. By making an increase in goods and services available to individuals and communities, we connect work and endeavour to wealth creation before they are swamped by economic measurement, fiscal measures or sociopolitical systems.

It is important for us to be challenged by the rich young man in the Gospels who was too attached to his possessions to take up the offer of eternal life. Jesus made it clear to him that his obsession with possessions was the enemy of his true freedom in this life as well as the next. He did not prosper in any full sense, since, as others have discovered, additional affluence does not automatically lead to happiness, and often leads away from it. Layard (2005) relates the cautionary tale of the King of Bhutan, who in 1998 made the enlightened announcement that his nation's objective would be the Gross National Happiness (GNH). A year later he made the fateful decision to lift a ban on multichannel television: a sharp increase in family break-up, crime and drug-taking followed.

Sociopolitical initiatives

International initiatives aimed at highlighting the challenges associated with sustainable development have featured repeatedly since the 1990s: the UN Conference on Environment and Development (UNCED) in 1992 (the Earth Summit), the UN World Commission for Sustainable Development in 1995, the UN General Assembly Special Session in 1997 (UNGASS or Rio +5), the UN Department of Economic and Social Affairs in 1998 (UNDESA), and the UN World Summit on Sustainable Development in 2002 (WSSD). Sustainable consumption and production rarely reach the headlines in any agenda, showing our reluctance to place them at the centre of discussions about sustainable development. In 2001, the Africa-led New Partnership for Africa's Development (NEPAD) committed African countries to a path of sustainable growth and development to halt marginalization of Africa in the globalization process and to enhance its full and beneficial integration into the global economy (http://www.nepad.org). This link between economic globalization and poverty eradication had been established earlier in India and China, but globalization has been largely adopted by the biggest players (the USA and EU) as a mechanism to increase their economic strength rather than place it at the centre of the global common good. As Churches Together in Britain and Ireland (2005) point out, this position is totally unacceptable and one that Christians must challenge by their insistence on a greater share of national wealth being used for the relief of poverty and debt relief, accompanied by greater political dynamism in respect of trade liberalization and ecological sustainability globally, since 'economic growth is by itself no guarantee of an absence of conflict, either internally or between nations, and growth gained unjustly can be a great threat to peace' (52).

Few documents, Christian or otherwise, relate the central significance of sustainable consumption and production (SCP) to the interests of the common good. There is a long way to go before SCP becomes more than a mental blueprint. In the UK, an encouraging sign is to be found in the Government's publication *Securing the Future* (2005), which details how Government departments are responding to the challenge of sustainable development. At least one, the Department for the Environment, Food and Rural Affairs, has begun to build an evidence-base and to construct indicators to evaluate whether economic growth and environmental damage can be decoupled, which will be essential if SCP is to move towards the centre of policy-making (DEFRA 2003).

Movement towards sustainable consumption and production demands more than administrative juggling. It must include a deeper understanding of the meaning of God's promise of the renewal of all creation through Jesus Christ; the application of our stewardship responsibility as depicted in the cosmic covenant; justice that addresses profligacy and poverty, which are at the epicenter of ecological and sociological catastrophes; equity that seeks to bridge the gaping divide between the more developed and less developed countries; and the development of a blueprint for sustainable consumption and production derived from the rich source of Christ's teaching. Achieving this will not be easy, but we must face the challenge for the sake of ourselves, our children and our grandchildren.

6. SUSTAINABLE ECONOMICS

Donald Hay

Donald Hay is acting Pro Vice Chancellor for Planning and Resources in the University of Oxford, and a Fellow of Jesus College. From 2000 to 2005 he was head of the Division of Social Sciences in the university, having previously taught in the Department of Economics. His research has been mainly in the field of industrial economics and organization. He was a contributor to the discussions that led in 1992 to the reform of competition policy in the UK, and was co-author of a major text on the subject, Industrial Economics and Organisation *(Oxford University Press, 2nd ed., 1991). He has long had an interest in the relationship between economic analysis and a Christian understanding of society, and is the author of* Economics Today: A Christian Critique *(Apollos, 1989).*

The aim of this chapter is both to inform and critique the approach taken by economists to sustainability problems. It reviews sustainability as approached by mainstream economists under three headings: (1) the situations in which issues of sustainability are thought to arise; (2) the (largely utilitarian) basis for economic evaluation of the sustainability issues, especially the discussion of intertemporal well-being; and (3) the range of policy prescriptions advanced by economists to counter threats to sustainability.

The context of this chapter is the Christian understanding of sustainability, as expounded by Dave Bookless in Chapter 2, which sets out two propositions:

1. The human race has been given a responsibility to act as stewards of the created order, to use it to sustain human flourishing, but not to despoil or destroy it. If we degrade the environment or use resources in a profligate manner, we are essentially depriving future generations of the ability to fulfil *their* role as stewards.
2. The environment has value, not just as the context in which the human race lives out its story. So an ecosystem that has no apparent value in terms of resources or economic activity nonetheless deserves protection and conservation.

From this starting point, this chapter shows how economists go about analysing the subject of sustainability. The first section lists a number of micro aspects, which require separate consideration: exhaustible resources, renewable resources, the exploitation of common resources, external effects in production and consumption such as atmospheric pollution, and the sustainability of ecosystems. We shall see that while the economic analysis and policy prescription for most of these is well developed, the analysis of the sustainability of ecosystems is not. Sustainability also has a macro aspect, arising initially from the Limits to Growth debates of the 1970s, which suggested that economic growth cannot continue indefinitely without the global economy running out of resources or the environment becoming utterly degraded (Meadows et al. 1972).

It has since been convincingly argued that these doomsday scenarios failed careful economic analysis because they did not incorporate the impact of resource scarcity on prices and the consequent incentives for substitution. However, they did draw attention to the importance of time in evaluating environmental sustainability and the rate of use of natural resources: the issue is how to address the trade off between the economic well-being of the current generation and the well-being of future generations. This leads to the second section and some very fundamental debates in economics about the basis for making such judgments and the degree to which the future should be discounted in deciding how many natural resources and capital stocks to leave for our successors. The third section surveys the policy approaches to tackle sustainability issues as proposed by economists.

A taxonomy of micro 'sustainability' problems

Economic analysis identifies a range of microeconomic 'sustainability' problems, which are qualitatively distinct even though the underlying analyses may have features in common (for a more detailed exposition of such problems, see Hay 1989: ch. 8). For the purposes of this chapter, these are taken as (1) exhaustible (or non-renewable) resources, (2) renewable resources, (3) the 'commons', as in the 'tragedy of the commons', (4) external effects in production or consumption, and (5) ecosystems and biodiversity, which are rather more 'macro' in their scope.

Exhaustible resources

It is self-evident that the earth's physical resources are finite and that problems will arise because certain resources are being used up at such a rate that they will be exhausted within the foreseeable future. The resource about which there is most concern is oil, since its exhaustion would appear to imply the loss of vital elements in our Western lifestyle, notably our use of cars and the use of hydrocarbons in manufacturing generally. Assume for the moment that the stock of a resource is indeed fixed and known. How will a market economy reflect that fact? The price of oil will increase over time at the market rate of interest. If the rate of price increase is less than the rate of interest, then it will pay firms to supply more now; if the rate of price increase is more than the rate of interest, then it will pay firms to keep the resource in the ground.

Given that prices in each period respond to supply and demand, the only equilibrium path of prices is one where the price increase equals the rate of interest. Assuming a positive rate of interest, the price of the resource will increase exponentially over time; assuming perfect foresight by industry, the path of prices will be set to exhaust the resource over its lifetime. For resources without substitutes, the lifetime is (technically) infinite, with ever-increasing prices and lower and lower rates of extraction. More plausibly, there will be substitutes that cost more, so eventually it pays users to switch. At that point in time the resource should be fully exhausted, since it is now worthless.

Four features of this price path are of interest:

1. The increase in the price of the resource over time represents an 'economic rent', reflecting the scarcity of the resource. That rent will of course generate returns for the owners of the resource that exceed the costs of extraction. If however there is no prospect of exhaustion of the resource, then the competitive market price will reflect only the costs of extraction, and there will be no rent.

2. The increasing prices give incentives to users to seek out substitutes, and to economize in their use of the resource by improving productivity. Increasing efficiency in the use of oil since the 1980s is a case in point.

3. The analysis assumes perfect foresight about the rate of use of the resource and the point at which it will be exhausted. If, as will generally be the case, there is imperfect understanding of the future, then the industry may be on the 'wrong' price path without knowing it, in the sense that the price is increasing at the rate of interest, but the general level is too high or too low, leading to a nasty surprise eventually, either when the resource is exhausted before a substitute is available, or when the industry is left with the resource unexploited in the ground.

4. The role of the rate of interest in the analysis. Firms will respond to market rates of interest: high rates will encourage use of the resource, while low rates will discourage it. But there are good reasons to believe that market rates will not fully reflect the views of the consumers. The appropriate interest rate should reflect the willingness of the current generation to save and invest for the future, including provision for generations

not yet born. Market rates will in practice reflect the views of the monetary authorities, and the risks attached by capital markets to investments for the future. The implication is that rates are probably too high, thus favouring current extraction and use rather than leaving the resource for future generations. The sustainability issue is therefore that we may be using up our resources too fast.

This gloomy conclusion depends on two quite strong assumptions: that it is impossible to substitute 'produced resources' for exhaustible resources in production, and that there is no scope for technical progress leading to more efficient use of exhaustible resources. Neither seems entirely plausible historically. Resource 'optimists' will claim that the path of increasing prices implied by the analysis will continue to stimulate substitution and technical change.

Renewable resources
The case of renewable resources is a bit more complex. A typical example is the population of an animal species in a geographically defined ecosystem. The relationship between the level of the stock and the growth of the stock is likely to follow an inverted U curve that cuts the horizontal axis (although stochastic rather than deterministic) (see figure below). If the initial stock is very low, the

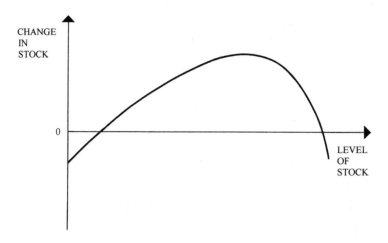

chance of finding a mate is small; if the chances of being killed by a predator are high, the stock will be on its way to extinction. With higher numbers, mating probabilities are higher, and there will be a tendency for the stock to grow. However as numbers increase, there will be pressure on the food supply. The stock will continue to grow over time until these two effects cancel out, indicating an equilibrium population for the species: any growth will be offset by food shortage and the stock will shrink again. The long-run equilibrium is stable.

Such a model also indicates the scope for 'farming' the resource. Growth in the stock can be harvested in each period, leaving the stock intact; the maximum take is at the peak of the curve. Note that numbers will be less than the long-run equilibrium: it is the tendency to grow towards the equilibrium value that creates scope for farming the resource in a sustainable manner.

The economic analysis of 'farming' renewable resources in a market context is complex, and all we can do here is sketch a number of possibilities. Imagine a fishing fleet in single ownership considering its policy for a fishing ground in which it is the sole operator. Assume the price of a catch and the costs of making a catch do not change with time. To maximize profits over time, the firm should reason as follows. Suppose the fleet makes an extra catch, and the firm invests the proceeds in government bonds. Then it can enjoy interest payments at the rate on bonds. Alternatively, it can forgo the extra catch, thereby slightly increasing the stock, and thus making possible slightly larger catches in future. The value of the incremental catches is in effect the return to the 'investment' represented by forgoing the catch now. An optimal policy will therefore involve decreasing the catch up to the point where the return on the 'investment' at the margin is equal to the interest rate; this is when the slope of the function relating growth to stock equals the interest rate. In practice, increasing the stock will make fishing less costly in the future as the fish are easier to find and catch; this return should be added to that of the investment in higher future catches.

Suppose now that the returns to forgoing the extra catch are small: increase in stock permits only slightly higher catches in the future, and there are no effects on costs. If the returns are lower

than the rate of interest, it always pays the firm to make the catch
now rather than invest in future catches. The profit-maximizing
policy will be to run down the stocks as fast as possible within the
constraints of the capacity of the fleet. The biological process is
just too slight to make it worth waiting for it to produce a natural
surplus.

If the industry consists of a large number of individual firms all
seeking their own advantage, the situation will be worse. The firms
may quickly destroy the stock; even if they know this is going to
happen, no one firm has an incentive to modify its behaviour on
its own. Given market demand for the fish, and the costs of
fishing, each firm seeks to maximize its own profits. If the activity
yields a surplus over costs, then more firms enter the industry until
the surplus is eliminated by a fall in the market price of the fish as
the landed catch increases. In general, the take depends on the
level of stocks. Higher stocks make fishing easier, and hence
cheaper. There are now two possibilities. In the first, the equilibrium take as a function of the stock is compatible with the
biological growth of the stock: this is the sustainable 'farming'
outcome. In the second, the equilibrium take exceeds the biological growth, and the stock is steadily fished out with the size of
the industry declining as the stocks decline. Unfortunately, this
second outcome cannot be attributed solely to the ignorance of
the firms concerning the biological dynamics. Suppose they have
been made fully aware the industry is sustainable only if their joint
take is reduced to the biological growth. An individual firm has
very little incentive to reduce its take: indeed, if it believes other
firms will reduce their take, its individual incentive is to increase its
own take, as that will be more profitable.

The 'tragedy of the commons'
The 'commons' are environmental resources not owned by
anyone. The problem is that unpriced external costs arise in the
use of these resources. Each user fails to take into account the
effect of his or her use on the availability of the resources to other
users, thus affecting their costs. The outcome is that at the margin
the returns to any one user are less than the social costs that fall on
other users. Textbook examples are common grazing grounds

where additional animals reduce the amount of fodder available to the animals already there, and fishing grounds where additional fishing boats raise the costs of the existing fleet as the fish become more scarce. The point is that individual agents have no economic incentives to restrict their activities, since they do not have to consider the costs they impose on others. This compounds the problems identified above. In the fisheries example, it increases the total take from the stock in each period, and makes it more likely that the take will exceed the biological growth associated with that stock, thus leading to irreversible decline.

External effects in production and consumption

External effects in production and consumption share some of the characteristics of the 'commons' but without the rivalry in resource use. The textbook examples are air pollution, where the activity generates costs experienced by others, and noise pollution, such as that suffered by people living near to airports. The problem here is that markets for such 'bads' do not exist, so the activities that generate them do not have to carry the full costs. The lack of markets is usually attributed to the lack of property rights in such things as a clean and quiet environment. Coase (1960) argued that the lack of such rights is not necessarily a problem: in his analysis, those who suffered from pollution and noise could in principle bargain with the activity-generating 'bads', offering to pay for a reduction in that activity to more acceptable levels. Alternatively, and intuitively with greater justice, the law could assign rights to clean air and quiet to the citizens, and the polluters would then have to negotiate with them over compensation. Or (for example) those affected could move or the polluters could invest in new technology to reduce the level of emissions. The problem with Coase's solution is the difficulty of coordinating the negotiations in a context where the external effects are suffered by a large number of people who have no single voice to speak for them. In practice, it is very unlikely that market outcomes will reflect the principles of Coase's analysis.

Ecosystems

Previous sections looked at 'sustainability' problems at the level of separate activities and markets. But it is very evident that the overall impact of such problems is greater than the sum of the parts, given that they interact globally or at least at the level of major ecosystems. We need to consider how the aggregation of problems generates whole-system issues before turning to a macroeconomic analysis. The most obvious example is that of climate change, where a combination of human activities (transport, heating and cooling of buildings, industrial production, agriculture, forest clearance) has contributed to increased levels of carbon dioxide and other greenhouse gases in the atmosphere, so that the cumulative impact is far greater than the sum of the contributions of those activities considered in isolation (see Chapter 3). It may therefore be appropriate to consider climate change issues as arising generally from economic growth. A second example is that of diversity in an ecosystem; we now know that modifying or removing a single element in an ecosystem can have dramatic effects on the other components of that system. The scope and variety of the effects makes it difficult to evaluate. Moreover the economic values to be assigned to the existence of an ecosystem or to preserving biodiversity are very unclear.

A macroeconomic analysis of sustainability problems

The macroeconomic analysis of sustainability focuses on two linked issues. The first is neatly captured by the definition in the Brundtland Report (World Commission on Environment and Development 1987: 43): 'Sustainable development is development that meets the needs of the present without compromising the ability of future generations to meet their own needs.' We need specifically to account for environmental assets, such as forests, water, air, species, rivers, seas and other natural resources, which are key determinants of the quality of life in many societies. The second issue is how we should handle the time dimension, where the long term is defined in terms of centuries, rather than decades.

Taking future generations into account

The nature of the 'trade offs' between current and future generations is a general issue for economic analysis, in the context of how much the current generation should invest in providing physical capital for future generations (Heal 1998: ch. 1; Dasgupta 2001: ch. 6). It has a specific application to the question of preserving environmental assets for future generations. The problem arises because in a market system only the current generation has a voice: by definition, future generations cannot enter markets to buy future options on a good, whether it is a consumer or an environmental good. Put cynically, 'Why should we do too much for future generations? After all, they will never do anything for us.' It must therefore depend entirely on the goodwill of the current generation towards future generations. One way in which this is expressed is the desire to leave assets to one's children and grandchildren. However, few people will consciously consider the welfare of several generations of their descendants, while some will either have no descendants or not care about the welfare of those they have. It would therefore be a mistake to rely on the bequest motive generally, and particularly so in the case of preservation of environmental assets that are common or 'public' goods rather than the subject of private bequests.

This raises the question of how much provision of physical capital – or conservation of natural resources – should be supplied to future generations as yet unborn. Economic analysis addresses this question primarily through the lens of utilitarianism. The assumption is that human well-being is determined by the level of consumption (net of the detriment of the effort required to produce the relevant goods and services). One proposal (the Ramsey formulation: see discussion in Dasgupta 2004: chs. 6–7) is that we should not distinguish in any way between generations: each generation is as entitled to well-being as every other generation. The key issue is whether we should introduce any discounting of the well-being of future generations. The Ramsey proposal is that we should not, since discounting implies that we give effectively zero weight to the well-being (consumption) of some distant future generations. However, if we live in a world with an indefinite future and many succeeding generations, then no discounting implies that more investment (refraining from consumption by saving) by the current generation could in principle provide benefits for a large number of subsequent generations, and would therefore require the current generation to save 'too much'.

One way of dealing with this is to introduce a notion of inter-generational equality, such that higher well-being in one period contributes to the overall sum of well-being across generations, but at a diminishing rate. The impact of this is to make it less advantageous to provide additional well-being to future generations via saving and investment, since the increase in their well-being will be weighted less highly than the loss of well-being of the current generation. A particular version of this way of looking at the matter is the Rawlsian criterion,[1] which is to choose the set of economic policies that maximizes the well-being of the least well-off generation. The difficulty with applying this criterion is evident in the case of a very poor country. If the objective is to maximize the well-being of the poorest generation, then that is likely to be the current generation, so there can be no savings to generate economic development and growth. The country is then trapped in a low-income equilibrium indefinitely, since each generation looking forward in turn is likely to be the poorest.

An alternative approach, but within the Ramsey framework, is to assign a higher weight to the well-being of the current generation than to the well-being of future generations. In ethical analysis, this corresponds to 'agent relative' ethics, rather than the strict impartiality of utilitarianism or Rawls's 'veil of ignorance'.[2]

---

1. Rawls developed his criterion on the basis that if we do not know what our level of well-being will be in any prospective state of the world, we should look for outcomes that give the maximum income to the poorest person, just in case it turns out that we are that poorest person. Our ethical point of view is therefore based on having to decide behind a 'veil of ignorance' as to how we shall be placed. See Rawls 1971.

2. This approach generates an analytic problem in that the ethical evaluations of particular distributions of well-being over time are incongruent. The current generation assigns a lower weight to the well-being of the next generation than the next generation will assign to its well-being once it is in charge of intertemporal resource allocation. Of course, an intelligent set of policy-makers in the current situation will be fully aware of this revision of the weights by the subsequent generation, and will take account of it in setting their policy.

However, there are fundamental objections to agent-relative ethics in this context. For individuals it may be acceptable, though not to be applauded, that they give greater weight to themselves than to others. But as a guide to policy it is no good at all: it is the responsibility of policy-makers to consider not just the current generation, but also the long-term implications for the economic well-being of the society they serve. The whole point is that they should act to safeguard the interests of future generations, which have no voice in current markets in determining the levels of saving and investment. Indeed, individuals may well hold incompatible views about the future: as consumers they may implicitly value their current well-being more highly than that of future generations, but as citizens they may vote for green measures that to be effective have to impinge on their current consumption.

Reflecting on the fact that in practice societies do discount future consumption by having positive real interest rates, economists have suggested three reasons why the well-being of future generations should be discounted by policy-makers:

1. 'Impatience' or 'pure time preference', which is a preference for jam today compared to an equal amount of jam tomorrow: while this makes some sense for an individual, who may be sufficiently unsure about his or her future preferences to discount, it makes much less sense for a whole society.
2. The non-zero probability that society as we know it (or even the whole earth) could come to an end (war, impact with an asteroid, catastrophic global warming): discounting the future reflects an 'eat, drink and be merry for tomorrow we die' attitude.
3. The empirical fact that succeeding generations have, for several centuries now, enjoyed an increasing level of consumption reflecting economic growth due to increasing skills, higher stocks of physical capital, and technological change. This might make us less concerned to provide for our successors, comforted by the thought that they are likely to be richer than us anyhow.

There are three counterarguments to the practice of discounting. Already mentioned is that any positive discount rate implies that we do not give any weight to the well-being of generations beyond some future date. The second is that the choice of discount rate has a critical importance in deciding policy responses (Weitzman 1998; Newel & Pizer 2000). A high rate could imply that we should not be too concerned with the effects of global warming a hundred years from now; a low rate gives much higher significance to long-term effects, and would indicate a need to take action quickly. There is some interesting evidence which shows that the discount rate that individuals apply declines with futurity. Very roughly, the implicit individual discount rate is on average 15% over the next five years, 10% over ten years, 5% over thirty to fifty years, and 2% over a hundred years. This suggests that applying a single discount rate is inappropriate, if the views of citizens are taken into account. The message is that people are concerned about the very long run, but also give a high weight to their consumption in the immediate future. The third objection is to the use of the discount rate to capture the risk of demise of the society. If the concerns are about truly catastrophic whole-society risks rather than more limited issues of sustainability, then expected values scarcely capture the scale of the problem.

This discussion no doubt appears unduly abstract to those concerned with practical issues of environmental sustainability. But it does serve to focus on the need to define our willingness to sacrifice our own well-being for future generations, and our reaction to societal risks that may be catastrophic.

Sustainable growth paths

The economic analysis of sustainability has generally been conducted in the context of growth paths for the economy. Why have most economists rejected the Limits to Growth forecasts (Meadows et al. 1972) for the world economy in the context of *non-renewable resources*? As explained above, the two main escape routes are substitution and resource-saving technical change, both of which are stimulated by the trajectory of prices for an exhaustible resource. There are actually two other effects that may extend the horizon for using up a non-renewable resource. The first is that the available reserves, for example of oil, are themselves a function of the price. A high price will make it worthwhile

to extract more oil from fields that were thought to be exhausted
at lower prices, because the costs were too high to justify continuing extraction. The oil fields of the North Sea are a good example
of this response. The second effect, though obviously not in the
case of oil, is that a higher price encourages recycling, thus extend-
ing the availability of the resource. The combination of these
effects with particular substitution and resource-saving technical
change has led most economists to reject the scenarios of the
Limits to Growth school. There does seem to be enough of both
substitution and resource saving to ensure that the growth rate is
not affected materially.

A slightly different way of looking at this problem is in terms of
what consumption path can be sustained in perpetuity (or consumption per head in a growing population). The classical analysis
of this problem provided a definition of sustainable consumption
as 'the maximum consumption that is compatible with maintaining capital intact'. In the context of exhaustible resources,
Hartwick's (1977) analysis showed that a sustainable consumption
path requires an amount of saving and investment in each period
equal to the market value of the current use of exhaustible
resource. The intuition is that the resource is equivalent to capital
stock, which, if used up in a period, must be replaced if income
and consumption are not to fall. This model presupposes that the
resource stock being used up can be effectively replaced by other
capital stocks.

In principle, the same analysis applies to a renewable resource,
as described above, where the rate of biological renewal is so low
that the optimal policy for firms is to run the stock down, rather
than seek to farm it.[3]

But the application of this analysis to *environmental goods* is highly
contentious. Various objections can be offered. The first is that
many environmental goods (e.g. clean air, clean water, and natural
landscape) are not traded in markets in the same way as exhaustible
resources like minerals, so the incentives for substitution and

---

3. If a renewable resource can be farmed, then in the long run it raises no
    problems for sustainability.

resource saving are absent. A second is that it is debatable to what extent environmental resources can be fully substituted by other produced resources. For example, is it really the case that chopped-down trees can be 'replaced' by an equal value of houses on the site? There is surely an additional loss relating to our enjoyment of the trees themselves. Such objections have led environmental economists to propose an amendment to the standard societal economic objective function by including the stock of environmental goods valued for its own intrinsic contribution to well-being, and with very restricted scope (or no scope at all) for substitution by produced goods or resources.

Using this amended objective function generates an additional twist to the analysis of optimal consumption paths over time. The rule is that the stock is used up until the point at which the extra utility attached to a marginal increase in consumption involves using up environmental goods equal to the present value of the stream of benefits from leaving the stock intact. In other words, the society initially uses up some of the stock, then stops, and from that point on the stock is maintained intact. A Rawlsian perspective requires zero consumption of the stock over time. If the stock is depleting over time the 'last' generation will have no stock at all, and will therefore be the poorest: their interests are best addressed by not consuming the stock at all.

The central question is *substitutability*, and this is an empirical problem (see Pezzey & Tomin 2002, especially sect. 4). With respect to *substitution in resources for production*, the issue is whether there are any limits to the effective substitution of new resources for non-renewable resources currently being used up. Note that substitutability is defined here to include technical change that improves the efficiency of resource use: the logic is that knowledge and human capital are being used to substitute material resources in production to produce the same outputs. 'Optimists' – who include the economics mainstream – argue that experience supports their optimism. In non-technical language, they claim, 'Don't worry too much about sustainability. The human race has proved itself highly adaptable in the past, and will in all probability be able to cope with whatever the future holds.' Optimists note, for example, that there is no sign of sharply increasing real prices for either renewable or non-renewable resources. This could be because the point in time at which they are expected to 'run out' is too far in the future to affect the current price, or because of the availability of substitutes (either produced or natural), or because of technical progress currently improving the efficiency with which the resources are used. This optimism even extends to issues like global warming, with the suggestion that climate change, even though rapid in comparison with the rates of change experienced in the last few thousand years, is sufficiently slow that one should expect technological adaptation to cope with it – cropping patterns will change, populations will retreat from low-lying coastal areas, and agriculture will learn to benefit from a warmer environment.

The 'pessimists' have a very different approach. Some pessimists appeal to the laws of thermodynamics. An implication of the first law is that the production of any material output requires an irreducible minimum input of material resource, so there has to be a limit to more efficient use of resources. Moreover, production inevitably generates by-products, and these residuals may be harmful to people and/or the environment. Counterarguments are as follows:

1. As economies grow richer, consumer demands for services grow much more than those for products, and services generally require fewer material inputs.
2. Recent economic history indicates steadily increasing productivity in the use of material inputs as the value added by human and knowledge inputs increases.
3. Material inputs, especially energy inputs, can be used to reduce the impact of residuals by reprocessing to render them harmless.

The second law of thermodynamics (the law of entropy) implies that production inevitably dissipates energy and materials that are concentrated or otherwise organized, so that degradation of natural resources is inevitable. The argument against this is that energy from the sun serves to recycle dissipated materials in biological cycles, and in principle we can utilize this energy to recover other wastes.

The resolution of these uncertainties has to be empirical. For example, can we capture enough energy from the sun to recycle materials effectively? And if the laws of thermodynamics eventually preclude further substitution, is this likely to occur within a time frame about which we need to take note?

Others argue against substitutability in production on the grounds of more fundamental principles. This can be termed 'strong sustainability'. The starting point is a rights-based argument that intergenerational justice imposes stewardship obligations on the current generation to preserve options for future generations. Destruction of an ecosystem will result in the loss of thousands of plants and species, and thus preclude our descendants from using those resources to do other things; for example, produce a drug effective against an infection the human race has yet to encounter. It is even possible, indeed likely, that future generations would be able to find better uses for fossil fuels than we have!

Three possible stances emerge from such considerations.

The first is the precautionary principle, which at its most radical would urge that we should not do anything to use up non-renewable resources or to destroy local ecosystems, so we can hand them on intact to our successors.

The second is that we should permit exploitation of natural resources and ecosystems only up to predetermined limits. Examples would be the setting of a target for concentrations of carbon dioxide and other greenhouse gases in the atmosphere, and the creation of forest reserves in the Amazon to be preserved in perpetuity. The practical problem is how to fix these limits in a way that is not essentially arbitrary. The ethical objection is that by allowing the current generation to pollute or degrade up to these limits, we are enjoying resources to boost our standard of living and denying the same opportunities to our descendants.

And thirdly, we should maintain the key functions of natural resource stocks by investing in renewable-based substitutes to match the inevitable declines in the availability of non-renewables (e.g. vegetable oils to replace petroleum). Note that this stance effectively concedes that at least some substitution is possible: if no substitution is possible, then presumably the non-renewable stock should not be touched.

All three stances fail to varying degrees to face up to the hard choices we might face in the future, particularly contexts in which we might wish to breach predetermined limits. Suppose humankind is facing a global infection that can only be curbed by using a resource available in an ecological reserve: it would be hard to argue that nonetheless the reserve should not be touched. There will always be trade offs to be evaluated.

We need also to address the issue of *substitution in consumption*. The simplest case involves the preservation of natural landscapes. The issue is simple to state but difficult to resolve: a trade off between maintaining the amenity of an area of natural beauty and sacrificing it in the interests of economic development. If the area is sacrificed, then consumers can no longer benefit; the issue is the degree to which their higher standard of living compensates for the loss. Standard economic analysis assumes that consumers can and do substitute between goods and services generally, but whether this extends to natural beauty is presumably an empirical matter. The 'strong sustainability' school of thought argues that even if our generation were willing to make the substitution for ourselves, we have a duty to leave the natural environment intact, rather than denying our descendants the option to enjoy it.

Promoting sustainability

The analysis of the first section above showed that there is not one sustainability problem, but a variety of micro problems. We must now examine the 'solutions' offered by economists, and then consider ways of looking at the aggregate of these sustainability problems, including an emphasis on consumption behaviour.

Exhaustible and renewable resources

The analysis of exhaustible resources such as minerals and petroleum, mentioned above, showed that the market price of an exhaustible resource rises exponentially at the market rate of interest as exhaustion approaches. This rise in price, it is argued, stimulates responses such as substitution, resource-saving technical change, greater efficiency in extraction, prospecting for new reserves and, where appropriate, recycling. It is an empirical question whether these responses are 'sufficient' in the sense of ensuring that the resource is not used up in a spendthrift manner. But a priori there is unlikely to be a need for policy measures in these cases.

Renewable resources such as forests, fish stocks and animals present greater problems. Above I sketched out an analysis in which such resources can be farmed without damaging the stocks in the long term. The trick is to restrict the take in each period to the rate of biological growth of the stock: this can be 'natural' growth, or in the case of agriculture and animal husbandry, biological growth stimulated by technological interventions (cultivation, fertilizers, pest control, breeding, genetic modification). Unfortunately, in a market economy a natural stock such as fish or forests may be at risk if the rate of biological growth is less than the prevailing interest rate. In that case, the most profitable option for the firms involved is to run down the stock and reinvest the proceeds in other productive activities that give higher returns than 'investing' in the conservation of stocks. This has been the fate of forests all over the world in recent years, and indeed historically was partly to blame for the deforestation of western Europe. It also explains to some extent the crisis of fishing stocks in European waters and off the north-east of the United States and Canada.

The solution to these problems has been to involve controls on either quantity or price. The former involves agreement between all the parties on the level of take compatible with the long-term sustainability of the stock. The European fisheries policy is such an approach, and illustrates vividly the problems involved in implementation (agreement on quotas, controls in the ports where the fish are landed, fleets belonging to countries not part of the agreement). The alternative is a tax on the take that raises the market price and reduces consumption to sustainable levels. Taxes are in principle easier to implement, but their effects are thought to be less predictable. So quotas are the preferred option.

The 'tragedy of the commons'
The tragedy of the commons was described above. The problem identified by economists is the lack of property rights in the

resource, leading firms to exploit the resource without regard to effects on others or on the overall resource stock. This compounds the problems identified for fishing and forestry in the previous subsection. The solutions advocated by economists are the same: licensing the firms that exploit the resources, setting quotas or introducing taxes to reduce consumption.

Dasgupta (2004: ch. 7.2) has suggested that in many traditional economies in the developing world these problems are solved organizationally. He quotes the dictum of Arrow (1974): 'Organizations are a means of achieving the benefits of collective action in situations where the price system fails.' There is certainly a key role for communities in protecting common property such as forests, grazing lands, local fisheries and water supply. Their effectiveness depends on social capital, in that access to a particular resource depends on membership of a local community. Cooperation in managing the resource may provide social capital for other community activities, such as marketing outputs, provision of schools and community meeting places, and security.

The picture is not however entirely rosy. Analyses of communities with common property in the developing world show that richer households take more than poor households from the commons: the explanation is that they have to be given a higher share to induce their continued cooperation in the collective. It is also the case that local commons are tending to be degraded in the developing world, suggesting that the organizations are failing. Possible reasons include instability due to civil unrest or community violence, rapid population growth, or immigration of settlers. The state may also be responsible: it may take measures to define property rights at the instigation of rich local landowners, introduce subsidies to promote the clearing of forest for agriculture, or support landowners against environmentalists (especially foreign 'experts') in the cause of development. It seems that communities are more likely to sustain commons where the local economy is largely non-market (traditional and subsistence); the introduction of opportunities to market the output quickly erodes the traditional economy, and with it the community management of the local commons.

External effects in production and consumption

The analysis of external effects has been part of the microecono-mist's tool kit for a long time, and a variety of approaches have been suggested. An economist's predilection, when faced with a market failure due to the absence of property rights, is to seek a means to create those rights, leaving the newly established market to sort out the problem. For example, if the problem is pollution of a water course by some upstream activity, then assigning prop-erty rights in clean water to those living downstream may enable a market in 'pollution' to arise where the polluter pays the polluted for the right to continue the activity to some level. However, there are unlikely to be many cases where this solution would work, as pollution is not usually geographically circumscribed, so it is difficult to assign property rights and even more difficult to create the necessary markets.

However, the standard alternatives are quotas and taxes (Helm 1998). With quotas the issues are how to determine their aggregate level, and how to ration them among the externality-creating activ-ities. The first requires not only an understanding of the science involved, but also a social cost-benefit analysis of the externality. It will seldom be the right solution to set a zero quota for the exter-nality: in principle, the policy-maker will want to balance the marginal social value of additional activity against the marginal cost of the externality. There may be other considerations in setting the quota: for example, the policy-maker may wish to encourage firms to invest in research and development to reduce the externality, and will determine a set of quotas that decline over time.

The second problem is the allocation of the quotas among the firms engaged in the activity. Just assigning these on the basis of recent levels of activity will seldom be the best solution: some firms may be in a better position than others to reduce the exter-nalities; and some firms may be producing products more highly valued than those produced by other ones. One solution would be to require firms to bid for 'externality' permits in an auction process: permits would go to those firms that had the highest-valued products and/or had little scope for reducing the externality they produce. Alternatively, the quotas could be assigned on the basis of recent activity, and then made tradable. Firms that can easily reduce emissions will then be willing to sell their permits to firms for whom the quotas are more valuable. The distinction between these two approaches is that the auction process generates revenue for the licensing authority, while allocation of tradable permits creates financial gains for firms able to sell their quotas without adding too much to their costs.

The alternative to quotas is a tax on the externality. Setting the level of the tax requires the same scientific and cost-benefit analyses as for quotas, but avoids the need to distinguish between firms. Each firm adjusts its own activity in the light of the new cost circumstances created by the tax. The authorities may announce a steadily increasing tax over time, in order to create incentives to firms to change their production methods. The tax solution, like the auction of quotas, has the advantage that it generates revenue for the authorities.

Ecosystems

I noted above that problems of climate change and the preservation of ecosystems involve more than the aggregation of the problems of renewable resources, the commons and externalities outlined above. Moreover, the analysis above has generally focused on issues and solutions that do not have an intertemporal aspect, whereas climate change and damage to ecosystems clearly do have intertemporal implications for the kind of world we shall leave to subsequent generations. In deciding what should be done, we cannot avoid the difficult questions about intertemporal well-being summarized above. To keep the discussion manageable, we shall take the issues of *aggregation* and *intertemporal effects* separately.

In respect of *aggregation*, Ehrlich (1968) introduced the concept of the 'environmental impact' of a society as the product of three elements: population, consumption per capita, and a technical coefficient that relates consumption to the impact measure. While it is unclear what might be an appropriate measure of aggregate environmental impact, the concept is useful for organizing our thinking about the issues. The technical coefficient captures all the diverse channels by which our consumption affects the environment, such as the use of exhaustible resources, the rate of attrition of renewable resources (rate of renewal too low, exploitation of commons), and additions to external effects that accumulate in the environment. In principle, the policy interventions described in the preceding subsections should, if successfully implemented, lower the coefficient and hence the impact. Just in terms of 'resource use' there is some evidence that the coefficient has fallen in recent decades, though whether this is due to policy is more debatable.

A report by the Sustainable Development Commission (2003) noted that in the period 1970–99, the GDP of the UK grew in real terms by 88%, while the 'total material input requirement' grew by only 12%. Greenhouse gas emissions remained stable over the same period because efficiency improvements in the use of energy just about kept pace with the growth in consumption. The report then noted that to meet the UK's international commitments on carbon emissions, the rate of technical efficiency gain would have to rise substantially above the levels achieved in recent decades, and that this was very unlikely. The report also identified the instruments available to policy-makers as targeted 'eco taxes' and incentives for the development of less environmentally harmful technologies.

An alternative interpretation of the technical coefficient focuses on consumer behaviour. As societies grow richer, and consumption per head rises, the proportion of income spent on services tends to increase. In general, services require fewer material inputs (including energy) for their production, so the coefficient falls. Consumers may also become more aware of environmental issues, and their preferences in consumption may shift towards goods that are produced with more environmentally friendly technologies. Economists tend to think that such shifts can be produced only in response to movements in relative prices, perhaps due to the imposition of environmental taxes. But there is some evidence that consumer awareness, and pressure on policy-makers resulting in 'green' legislation, can make a substantial difference.

Finally, it is obvious from Ehrlich's formulation that environmental impact can be lessened by reductions in consumption per capita. This has led some contributors to the sustainability debate to question economic growth, with rising consumption per capita, as an appropriate objective for economic policy. They object to the narrow focus of most measures of national income, partly because they fail to include other things such as the quality of relationships that contribute to human flourishing, and partly because they fail to account properly for environmental losses. These criticisms are clearly correct. It is hard to get agreement on how measures of economic output should be adjusted to allow for them. Note however that as far as environmental sustainability is concerned, impacts on the environment would certainly be reduced for a given value of Ehrlich's technical coefficient if consumption slowed. But if growth can be offset by steady reductions in the coefficient, the environmental impact is of less concern.

The second issue to be addressed is *intertemporal effects*, which we explored above. The nub of the question is how much we should leave to future generations, whether in the form of unused natural resources, or in the form of a pristine natural environment. Given current technologies, an increase in our current economic activity will use up more of our natural resources, and contribute to environmental change, with the consequence that succeeding generations will inherit fewer natural resources and a more degraded environment. The 'green' response to the question is to argue that we should stop using exhaustible resources, that we should stop exploiting renewable resources beyond the rate at which they can be farmed sustainably, and that all activities that contribute to global warming or degradation of ecosystems should cease immediately. The cost of introducing such a radical programme in terms of current living standards would be very substantial.[4]

As soon as one moves away from such radicalism, and allows some current 'using up' of resources, and some degradation of the environment, then one has to address the issue of the intertemporal trade offs. This involves not only evaluating the future growth paths of the world economy, given different rates of current activity and assumptions about evolution of the 'technical coefficient' of environmental impact; it also requires us to make

---

4. I have not seen the radical green programme fully evaluated in terms of
   its effects on current living standards in the UK.

decisions about the appropriate framework for evaluating the trade off between the level of well-being of current and future generations. As the second section above showed, this involves taking a view on the appropriate social discount rate, and on the degree to which natural resource stocks can be substituted by man-made capital stocks when it comes to human well-being. These are substantive issues. In the debate on global warming, for example, a high discount rate suggests we need not take much account of the impact in fifty or a hundred years, and so there is no need to act now, while a low rate implies immediate action. Equally, there can be very different views on whether the capital stock constructed (drainage, farm buildings, fences, roads) on a particular piece of land to prepare it for agricultural use is in any way a valid substitute for the forest cleared to make way for it. If some substitution is acceptable, then much greater exploitation of natural resources can be permitted.

These are matters of principle for which there are no easy solutions. However, there should be agreement that 'leaving it to the market' is unlikely to generate a satisfactory outcome. Market interest rates tend to be higher than most estimates of social discount rates, if only because the market rates incorporate premiums for private risks, which are of no concern to society as a whole. Moreover, environmental externalities are seldom reflected adequately, if at all, in the market prices of goods and services, though with appropriate environmental taxes or tradable permits they could be. Currently, the 'market' almost certainly gives incentives for too great exploitation of resources and for too much degradation of the environment.

Conclusions

This chapter began with two propositions drawn from Christian theological ethics that should inform our view of sustainability. These identified requirements to exercise our stewardship of the created order in such a way as to provide for succeeding generations to exercise their stewardship, and to protect and conserve that created order for its own sake. The economic analysis that followed can help us in the application of these propositions in three respects. The first is that 'responsible stewardship' requires an understanding of the variety of 'sustainability' problems that need to be analysed separately. The second is that these problems raise fundamental conceptual issues Christians must address, such as the weight to be given to the interests of future generations, the degree to which produced resources can substitute for natural resources, and the weight to be given to environmental resources that have no immediate economic value. The third respect is in the design of policies to achieve sustainability. Used appropriately, economic analysis can help us to convert our concern for our planet into actions that will sustain God's creation for future generations of responsible stewards.

© Donald Hay, 2007

7. A FRAMEWORK FOR SUSTAINABLE AGRICULTURE

John Wibberley

Professor E. John Wibberley, MA, MTh, MSc, PhD, FRAgS, is an agriculturalist and resource management consultant. His work has involved assignments in over thirty-five countries in all continents, especially Africa. He is a Visiting Professor at the Royal Agricultural College, Cirencester (where he was Head of Agriculture until 1989), Adjunct Professor at the University of Guelph, Canada, and, since 1994, Visiting Fellow in International and Rural Development at the University of Reading. Professor Wibberley serves as Facilitator to RURCON, an otherwise all-African team of Christian Development practitioners working since 1971 within sub-Saharan Africa, with headquarters in Nigeria. He is an international Nuffield Farming Scholar and has worked with Farmers' Groups for thirty years. He was Chairman of the UK Farm Crisis Network (FCN) from 1998 to 2003. He coordinates the Associateship and Fellowship award scheme of the UK Royal Agricultural Societies, which recognizes excellence in contributions to agricultural and rural progress in the UK. He is a past Chairman of the Agricultural Christian Fellowship.

Agriculture has an inherent potential for sustainability founded on its two great continuous cyclical processes: photosynthesis and decomposition (the latter achieved by respiration at cellular level, mainly aerobic but also, in some cases, anaerobic). While microbiology, and in particular biochemistry, are perhaps the most significant sciences undergirding agricultural processes, the concept of sustainability extends beyond them. Similarly, agriculture is a wide concept including agricultural sciences (which are concerned with molecules, cells, organisms, processes); farming practices, which focus on populations (crops, herds) and enterprises such as milk production; and agricultural economics involves systems, marketing, policies and world trade.

'Agriculture' as a term came into common usage in the seventeenth century. Its origin is the Latin *agricultura*, combining *ager* (land, field) with *cultura* (culture). The word 'culture' derives from *cultus* (cultivation) and *colere* (to till, to cultivate, to 'worship' – as in 'cult'). Thus the word 'agriculture' includes ideas of physical land, land as a total context for human activity, and land as spiritually significant (Brueggemann 2002). It is not simply about producing useful crops or livestock, though these are obviously key outputs.

Agriculture's biblically recorded origins may be traced to the fall (Gen. 3:17–19); this has the assumption that its practice is likely to remain a struggle until the restoration of garden conditions in the new earth (Rev. 21:1), which in Micah's vision will entail a safe place and removal of fear (Mic. 4:4). However, Christians are called to 'work' while the Lord is away (Luke 19:13) and to seek 'substantial healing now' as Francis Schaeffer (1968, 1973) put it. Schaeffer saw the contemporary despair and sense of meaninglessness as directly consequent upon the trend towards autonomous rationalism (i.e. making human reason the sole arbiter of everything). He traced the origins of this insidious movement to the false dichotomy between nature and grace propounded by Thomas Aquinas (who did not, of course, rule out revelation). Secularization through the Middle Ages steadily led to the natural overtaking the supernatural in the dominant world view. Thus it was that White (1967) famously indicted Christianity for propounding conquest of nature or legitimization of its exploitation through an unbiblical, uncontextualized interpretation of Genesis 1:28.

'Sustainability' is a relatively recent term in common usage, but its concepts are profoundly theological and ancient. The

Authorized Version of the Bible uses the terms 'sustain' (e.g. Pss 3:5; 55:22; Neh. 9:21) and 'sustenance' (e.g. 2 Sam. 19:32; Acts 7:11), while the word 'Jesus' (e.g. Luke 1:31) literally means 'God (Yahweh) saves' or 'God is Saviour'. While English has difficulty accommodating the continuous present tense, some other languages do not. In English, for instance, Ephesians 5:18 exhorts, 'be filled with the Spirit', as if this is a one-off event, whereas the Greek conveys the continuous present tense such that it really means 'be being filled with the Holy Spirit'. In the same way, 'Jesus saves' is often used in English as a one-off event like a rescue from drowning. In a sense, this meaning is valid, but the richer, more comprehensive meaning is that 'Jesus rescues and maintains in safety'. It is this continuous, comprehensive, long-term sense of the word 'sustainability' that is conceptually (and therefore practically) vital. 'Sustain' can thus be fully understood to mean 'held in safety' or 'upheld'. 'Sustenance' carries the idea of 'all necessary provision for the support of life'.

Agriculture needs such sustenance itself – not only for rescuing it from destruction (including perhaps self-destruction in the case of some systems), but also it needs revaluing and maintaining in a state of long-term safety in order to provide its diverse benefits to civil societies and the global environment (Curry et al. 2002). This must take on board greed, normally associated with excessive *consumption*, but needs also to be applied to the concentration of excessive *production* that deprives many of opportunity to produce, as well as creating other ethical and practical problems such as pollution.

Agricultural sustainability

Attainment of sustainability is vital internationally in order to maintain and deliver

- *conserved* biodiverse (species-rich) landscapes (already done by the best farmers);
- *'commonwealth'* integrated economies that maximize local interdependence;

- networks of *relational* communities (where good relationships are strengthened).

Sustainability is a comprehensive concept with at least twelve 'E' (essential) criteria (Wibberley 1989, 2003a), which must simultaneously satisfy the following:

1. *Economy*: managing all creation's resources for the benefit of all creation.
2. *Ecology*: balanced care of the environment and its associated flora, fauna and people.
3. *Equity*: pursuit of justice for all in a shared earth of shared wealth, *not* shared poverty.
4. *Energy-efficiency*: wasting less energy in farming and food delivery systems.
5. *Employment*: promoting creative employment to secure local farm product supply.
6. *Ethics*: guidance to do what is good, fair and right in relation to God's perspective.

All these require e-promoters: *education, enterprise, enthusiasm, effort-effectiveness* with *expectancy* of some reward/success leading to *enjoyment* of living on a worldwide basis. These may be put together in the context of the cross:

e	E	e
E	E	E
e	E	e
e	E	e

These twelve Es can be used as a kind of template or checklist against which a particular agricultural, or indeed maritime (Clover 2004), system may be evaluated. In general, if this is done, it is very difficult to escape the conclusion that the thrust driving agriculture worldwide has to change. Present policy, especially that of the World Trade Organization on trading, is patently not sustainable for farmed or wild species, for farmers or for consumers in general. However, many agricultural systems delivering sustainability already exist in practice

(King 1911; Duckham & Masefield 1970; Joy & Wibberley 1979; Pretty 2002; Mortimore 2005). Good farmers merit greater respect.

The Bible raises ethical dilemmas in relation to sustainable agriculture. On the one hand, it exhorts a pilgrim attitude in our earthly lives – a journeying, nomadic, provisional approach. Yet it also encourages the planting of gardens and portrays blessing as a settled state. We have to hold these in creative tension. In the biblical world view, we are tenants only of this earth (even if in Roman law we have a freehold title to land). When we live unsustainably, we are, as the USA bumper sticker has it 'having fun spending the grandchildren's inheritance'. As an approach to these dilemmas, it is useful to study the incredible sustainability over millennia of the nomadic lifestyle found in both East and West Africa before population pressure (mainly from sedentary surrounding peoples and settlers) restricted the movement of pastoralists. We need to integrate five models proposed in Scripture for our relationship with creation:

1. *Dominion*: 'complete authority' to do what God likes with creation, not to dominate it! (Gen. 1:26–28).
2. *Priesthood*: the role to let creation express itself in praise to God (Ps. 150:6) and to offer it to God with praise.
3. *Companionship*: respectful, caring relationship with creatures (Prov. 12:10).
4. *Stewardship*: accountable, caring management of resources (Luke 16:2).
5. *Teamwork*: co-workership in team effort, with God (1 Cor. 3:9).

Sustainable agriculture features certain guidelines and field practices:

- Good soil conservation that also achieves (and can be promoted as) good water catchment.
- Feeding the soil by recycling nutrients and maintaining growth-conducive soil conditions.
- Mixing and/or rotating crops of different plant families to limit weeds, pests and diseases.
- Reduced and timely cultivations with correct spacing and depth of planting for each crop.

- Integrating livestock to use crop by-products and to produce manures or enrich composts.
- Use of human urine is an opportunity, and faeces can also be composted (but with great care).
- Encouraging the sharing of experience and wisdom of local farmers for mutual progress.

If one is among the over 800 million (some 12% of the world population) who are hungry, sustainable agriculture has a very poignant and immediate meaning. One practical approach towards addressing this challenge is summarized within case study 1.

Three case studies

Case study 1: conservation farming

Conservation Agriculture is defined by the Africa Conservation Tillage Network (set up at the University of Zimbabwe in Harare in 1998 and supported by German aid through the German Agency for Technical Cooperation) as 'the simultaneous practice of minimal soil disturbance, permanent soil cover and crop rotations/associations'. It involves zero tillage, first tried in the USA in the 1930s, in the UK during the 1960s and in Zimbabwe during the early 1970s. As a direct result of applying his Christian faith, conservation farming (CF) was developed from 1982 by Brian Oldreive (Oldreive 1993) at Hinton Estates, Bindura, Zimbabwe, and expanded to cover 3,840 hectares of annual crops by 1994, when he had already set up fifty trial plots on small farms nationwide. His experience has led him to be convinced of the validity of CF for all areas of Zimbabwe, except the very sandiest soils of the Kalahari fringes.

Oldreive was invited to Zambia by the World Bank to share his findings in 1995, and the development of CF accelerated rapidly in that country. In Zambia, the Conservation Farming Unit sets out the following principles: 'no burning of residues; correctly spaced permanent planting basins established before the rains; early planting of all crops; early weeding; rotation with a minimum of 30% legumes in the system'. As to fine-tuning these principles, best practice in farming is always location specific, especially with regard to soil and climatic conditions. Tropical farmers, especially those marginalized in the most vulnerable areas, are risk averse in order to be survival oriented. This often leads to fatalism followed by defeatism. CF can offer a way out of this vicious circle of poverty.

A central philosophy of CF is to 'feed soil' and so build fertility over time. Some key points about it are as follows:

- CF incorporates many timeless concepts of good husbandry. It links reduced early cultivation, seed and nutrient placement, mulching and rotations. African and other tropical farmers traditionally practice shallow cultivation anyway.
- CF with a two-year agroforestry rest (of *Sesbania sesban, Tephrosia vogelii*) is used by the International Council for Research in Agroforestry. In Zambia, alternating a year of sunn hemp (*Crotalaria*) is being tried, as are interplanted trials on *Faidherbia (Acacia) albida* at 100 trees per hectare. (It is in leaf in the dry season, thus reducing its competitiveness to field crops, and can fix 300 kg of nitrogen per hectare.)
- 'Zero tillage', 'no-till', 'minimal cultivations' are 'Western' terms for 'mechanized plus herbicides' ways of least-cost minimal tillage.
- CF offers a disciplined, adaptable management approach for all (not a fixed 'package'). It is 'sustainable agriculture', but precise management obviously varies.
- CF uses zero or low-cost input, including the opportunity cost of farmers' dry season time.
- CF can easily use organic and inorganic fertilizers with hand, animal or tractor power.
- Minimal cultivation may change weed ecology, needing more initial in-crop weeding (with maybe more perennials, which may later warrant a chemical herbicide). Weed control is critical in all systems, but CF can use the 'opportunity cost' of farmers' labour if this is mobilized in a disciplined way.
- CF saves energy by moving only some 15% of soil by contrast with overall tillage.
- West African Sahel experience suggests CF 'basins' can boost yields from double to tenfold. Having enough labour for dry season land preparation and ample weeding is important.
- On heavier soils in Malawi, excess January rain in basins can

lower CF yields and give little mulch for future crops. Some CF crops there need weeding as many as six times.
- In the Indo-Gangetic Plain (an area of 13.5 million hectares, the world's most intensively farmed region, which produces 45% of South Asia's food), 0.5 million hectares have been conservationally farmed since 1999 with support from the Department of International Development. In that region, wheat and upland rice are now zero-tilled: wheat yields are up 10–17% with cost savings of £70–100 per hectare.

Keys to conservation farming success in Zambia
Apparent reasons for the estimated adoption of CF by over a hundred thousand Zambian farmers on at least part of their land are as follows:

1. It has been practical, farmer led and developed.
2. There is a motivated extension team of some forty people (though less than one-third are female, despite some 85% of farm work being done by women).
3. Adequate fertilizer has been used to get good yields (including of mulch residues); on-farm yields of up to 9 tonnes per hectare of maize and 3.5 tonnes per hectare of cotton have been attained.
4. Appropriate technology has been introduced (including the *Chaka* hoe, *Magoye* ripper, *Zamwipe* weeder and *Teren* rope marker – with spaced bottle-caps to mark plant stations).
5. There has been good liaison with field research/practice (e.g. Research Stations, Organic Centre, Seed Inoculant Company).
6. Biodiversity has been encouraged with location-tested cropping systems.
7. Farmer-to-farmer adoption is encouraged – already over a hundred thousand are doing some CF largely through emulating neighbours (Farmers' Study Groups could multiply this effect).
8. The Zambia National Farmers' Union and the Government have endorsed CF.
9. The Conservation Farming Unit has had international donor support, it has produced excellent promotional materials and has kept its focus on agronomic management and extension

(liaising with other organizations regarding matters such as crop storage, marketing and nutrition).

10. Headmen in villages allocate land for use and have become key promoters for CF.

11. Neighbours help each other in fieldwork and discuss their CF experiences together.

Case study 2: genetically modified crops

This can be only a brief summary of an increasingly topical subject (for a fuller treatment, see Bruce & Bruce 1998; Bruce & Horrocks 2001; Wibberley 2003b). I hope it will serve sufficiently to illustrate the dilemmas, pros and cons of the issue. Livestock and human genetically modified (GM) uses arguably pose greater ethical dilemmas than GM use in crops (although GM-derived drugs for human use have been largely non-controversial, as with insulin for diabetes or clotting factor for haemophilia).

The case for genetically modified crops

- Multiple gene copies can be made easily for desirable characteristics.
- Rapid breeding can accelerate the provision of improved crop varieties.
- Wide species choice: genes from virtually anywhere can be drawn upon.
- Reduced chemical use? Practice so far does not quite live up to expectations.
- 'Nutraceuticals': scope to make medical, pharmaceutical and nutritional products.
- Stress resistance: to adapt crops to survive dry, saline or other harsh environments.
- Feed the world? Scope to increase output by breeding adaptable high-yield varieties.

The case against genetically modified crops

- Boundaries between species? God created everything 'after its kind'.

- Safety? Meddling with components may threaten those of high allergenic susceptibility.
- Environment: once released, how to recapture or control destinations is problematic; cross-contamination into weeds related to out-pollinating species is an issue (e.g. charlock with oilseed rape).
- Control: this is already alarmingly supranational and not subject to normal national regulation.
- Commoditization: already accelerating (e.g. fastfood GM soya and maize inclusions).
- Alternatives: sustainable, high-yield, energy-efficient, non-GM farm systems exist.

GM needs to be approached in a strictly limited, cautious way.

Case study 3: sustainable agricultural trading management

International trade is the subject of much confused thought, policy and practice. Excessive trading is perhaps the greatest general threat to agricultural sustainability. Micah 4:4 (everyone under their vine and their fig tree and no-one making them afraid) succinctly expresses the opposite of what many farming families experience, although it is an appropriate aim in international development for as many as possible. Local earth-care, sustainable livelihoods and food security are keys to greater world stability through justice, peace and the integrity of creation. These must go together in *each place*, yet are hugely threatened by indiscriminate trading.

How then might sustainable trading management be achieved – notably for agricultural products?

1. The trade-related intellectual property (TRIP) rules enable 'biopiracy' and threaten access to traditional knowledge for farming communities (Shiva 2000). We should seek international agreement to change the World Trade Organization policy of non-discrimination against imports, negotiating and substituting a 'Highway Code for Trading'. Associated with this, we need to raise public awareness in every country of the livelihood, environmental and defence importance of buying locally grown foods as much as possible. Landscapes should be both

beautiful and good for food everywhere; farmers in place are the cheapest and most practicable way this can be delivered throughout the world. Biology, not financial speculating, must govern food supply.

2. Challenge trade involving the delivery of products to countries where they could be grown already. For example, much rice in many African countries is unnecessarily and damagingly coming from Asia. Chickens are being traded around the world when they can be raised easily in most countries; South American and Asian chicken is destroying poultry enterprises in Africa. Cheap North American cotton is ruining cotton farmers' livelihoods in West Africa. To suggest that, following debt cancellation, Africa join in the trading spree as an assured route to prosperity is as naive as it is disastrous: livelihoods, environmental quality and food security are all at stake.

3. Encourage fair-trade policies product-by-product, as a prelude to an internationally agreed fair-trading context. (Removal of agricultural products from the World Trade Organization policy has been proposed, which would offer immediate help, but trading in other products can be excessive and thus needs more moderation; Tudge 2004.)

4. Maximize the processing of export products within their countries of production (e.g. groundnuts into peanut butter *in situ*, solar-drying of tropical fruits, processing of beverage crops). Sugar from temperate and tropical sources (beet, maple, cane) should be grown in the appropriate countries; UK sugar beet is a rotationally beneficial crop that requires deep soil management, which encourages game birds and other wildlife as well. Simply to import cane sugar into the UK as our sole source does not make sense, despite higher energy-capture of cane in field.

5. Encourage development of biofuel crops for renewable energy near sites of need.

6. Encourage farmers to form FARMS (Farm Asset Resource Management Study) groups, where they meet from farm to farm and learn together. They may come to learn together as trust develops from sharing of ideas and experiences into sharing of purchasing, of equipment use and of selling for local agricultural progress everywhere.

Conclusion

Some agri-theology principles for sustainable agriculture can be derived from the foregoing (Gorringe & Wibberley 2002):

1. God is Creator and Sustainer of the universe.
2. Human beings are created in God's image and designed for right relationships: *up* (God), *out* (neighbours) and *down* (earth). Only an integrated person can achieve this (Ps. 86:11).
3. All creation is fallen through sin, but creation shares in Christ's salvation.
4. Agriculture is stewardship of creation for food and primary products; farmers are human stewards; greed can apply equally to production and consumption.
5. Rural development needs to provide capacity to *care* for creation (e.g. know one's beasts, Prov. 12:10), *share* with those who do not have enough, *work* in harmony with God (1 Cor. 3:9), *be in place* (relate locally to land and community), *access enough* (avoid excessive expansion, Isa. 5:8).
6. Christian ethics are required in agriculture to reconcile simultaneously *economy*, *ecology*, *energy-efficiency*, *equity* and *employment*.
7. Agriculture is a vocation, since earth is God's farm.

All this needs advocacy to integrate sustainable farm livelihoods, natural resource management, food security and land heritage connections everywhere. Farmer conservation coupled with the encouragement of farmer collaboration is crucial; practical farmers have the integrated realism to be well placed to implement these interdependent pursuits (Wirzba & Kingsolver 2003). Sustainable agriculture requires collective humility and repentance, followed by disciplined farming that brings 'healing to the land' (2 Chr. 7:14; see also Jung 2005).

© John Wibberley, 2007

8. LET JUSTICE ROLL DOWN LIKE A NEVER-ENDING STREAM

Joanne Green

Joanne Green works as the Advocacy Manager for Progressio (previously called the Catholic Institute for International Relations), an international development charity working for justice and the eradication of poverty. Before moving to Progressio, she was the Senior Public Policy Officer on water and sanitation at Tearfund. During that time, Joanne was seconded for six months to work for the UK Department for International Development as Policy and Civil Society Advisor.

Water is life . . . and death

All around the world, water rituals are happening. An old man fills up the kettle. A toilet flushes. A small girl sets out on a long walk, jerrycan in hand. A sparrow dips its head into a birdbath, shaking droplets of water over its body. A young man splashes cold water on his face after a shave. A mother washes clothes in a stream. A priest pours water over a screaming baby's head. A tired office worker lowers her body into a hot lavender-scented bath. A school-boy jumps over a stagnant pool of water outside the corrugated shack he lives in. Cattle slurp. A golf course sprinkler refreshes a green. A jogger stops for a long gulp of iced water.

As I write, south-east England is gripped by its worst drought in thirty years and we are faced with the prospect of what millions of people do all over the world every day – queuing for water. In the normal run of things, we don't even think about water; water creates very few headlines, such is the regularity of supply and ease of use. But as soon as there's too much or not enough, news-papers shriek and politicians complain.

Water is integral to every part of our life: from the political, cul-tural, social, recreational, environmental and religious to our obvious physical needs. All life is dependent on water. God made water an integral part of creation. He created it in abundance: flowing streams, roaring waterfalls, winding rivers, majestic lakes all signal God's lavish nature, his unstinting generosity, his celebra-tory joy in creating life and giving it to us to look after.

But, as Romans 8 puts it, creation is groaning. Our dependence on water for everything brings with it a curse. People use water to wield power over others. Often there isn't enough water or there's too much of it and it isn't there at the right time, in the right place. Water has even become sinister – as a vector and breeding ground for disease.

All this manifests in four main ways, through

- the availability and quality of water itself;
- our mismanagement of the resource by pollution and overexploitation;
- governments failing to provide drinking water and sanitation for their citizens because of problems outside and within their control; and
- those in power using their control of water sources to subject others to their will.

Poverty and the environment are inextricably linked. Water shows, perhaps more profoundly than any other environmental issue, our dependence on natural resources for poverty reduction and sustainable development. We cannot address poverty and injustice, unless we also manage our natural resources in a just and sustainable way. God's response can be summed up in two essential hallmarks of his coming kingdom – stewardship and justice.

The planet

Water is all around us: in the air, on the surface of the earth and underground. The hydrological cycle is 'the global mechanism that transfers water from the oceans to the surface, or subsurface environments, and plants, to the atmosphere that surrounds our planet' (UNESCO 2006: 139). Only about 3% of the world's water is freshwater and most of that is locked up in glaciers and ice sheets, with the result that only about a quarter of it is accessible for human use.

We are often given the impression that growing water scarcity is outside our control and any shortage is simply nature's whim. This is simply not the case. Scarcity is almost always caused by bad governance – a failure to manage water sustainably and justly. This hits poor people the hardest. Water can be a renewable resource, but pollution and unsustainable exploitation of fresh water and associated ecosystems (using water faster than it naturally replenishes) reduces the amount and quality of water available to us.

During the twentieth century, water consumption increased sixfold, twice the rate of population growth. Allowing for increase in numbers, the UN Commission on Sustainable Development have calculated that two out of every three people will be living with water shortages by 2025; at the moment one-third experience water shortages.

Surface water

Most surface water is in lakes as distinct from streams, rivers, reservoirs and wetlands. Many lake ecosystems in low- and middle-income countries are in decline. Lake Chad in West Africa and Lake Victoria in East Africa are two of the most cited cases. Satellite pictures of this dramatic decline are truly terrifying. From 1963 to the mid-1980s Lake Chad shrank over tenfold, from approximately 23,000 square kilometres to less than 2,000 square kilometres. Its fish populations were a crucial source of nutrition for, and central to the livelihoods of, the communities around it.

Many large mammals (such as elephants and hippopotami) live in the surrounding wetlands.

The major reason for the lakes shrinking is extraction of water for irrigation. This has been aggravated by overgrazing and deforestation making the regional climate drier. Local communities have suffered from major crop failures, livestock deaths and the collapse of local fisheries. All of this has contributed to increased poverty in the region (UNESCO 2006). After severe droughts in the 1960s to 1980s, Lake Chad began to recover a little. But the Intergovernmental Panel on Climate Change (IPCC) predicts decreased rainfall patterns and the return of more frequent droughts.

'Water saturated environments' such as bogs, swamps, mangroves and marshes, which collectively make up 'wetlands', are probably the least appreciated and understood of watery ecosystems. The wetlands of Iraq are perhaps the best known – both for their destruction and their subsequent rehabilitation (Richardson et al. 2005). Globally, many wetlands have been converted to farmland and severely degraded, particularly in South-East Asia.

MOPAWI, an indigenous Christian organization and Tearfund partner in western Honduras, is working with local poor communities in the Man and Biosphere Reserve of Río Plátano (Rand 2000). The reserve includes a variety of wetlands and is recognized by UNESCO as a World Heritage Site because of its exceptional ecosystem diversity. The area is home to three indigenous groups: the Miskito, Pech and Tawahka. They eke out a living through a variety of activities including agriculture, hunting and fishing, and use the forest for firewood, timber for construction of houses and canoes and medicinal plants. Many Miskito communities live on a thin ribbon of land between the sea and the Ibans Lagoon, the second largest lagoon in the reserve. This strip has come under increasing pressure through population growth and the immigration of landless farmers, leading to deforestation, overfishing, sedimentation, soil and water pollution, and, most worryingly, erosion. It used to be protected by mangroves and other vegetation but these have been cleared for firewood, to create space to build houses, for boat landings and to provide access to the lagoon for bathing and washing clothes. As a result, wave action during bad weather repeatedly erodes the area. This was particularly bad during Hurricane Michelle in 2000, when sea water contaminated the lagoon and made it unusable for most domestic purposes.

MOPAWI has been working very closely with the local communities to re-establish the mangroves and so reduce erosion and improve the habitat for fish. They have also been working with the locals to help them find ways to manage waste and resources sustainably. The experience shows the dependence of the villages on healthy ecosystems. Planting living fences to protect the mangroves against human interference has been particularly successful because these fences do not rot or suffer from termites. Even though poverty was a factor contributing to the original ecosystem degradation, working closely with the communities helps to develop sustainable solutions to manage their resources (Collins, unpublished case study: 'Community Led Management and Protection of Shared Natural Water Resources: The Case of Ibans Lagoon, La Mosquitia, Honduras').

Groundwater
Incredibly, groundwater (water stored beneath the world's surface) represents 96% of accessible fresh water; it is the origin of much surface water, feeding springs, wetlands and streams. It too is under immense pressure. Overpumping of groundwater by the world's farmers exceeds natural recharge rates by at least 160 billion square metres per year. In the Ganges delta, increased drawdown of the water table because of overpumping for irrigation has destroyed the effectiveness of the simple shallow pumps used to draw water for domestic use from the thousands of tubewells in the countryside (Postel 1999).

Impact on agriculture
At least 70% of water used by humanity is for agriculture. Globally, the total amount employed for this purpose is increasing, partly because of population growth but more importantly because rich and middle-income countries are eating more meat, the production of which requires more water than cereals and vegetables. The amount of water needed to grow one kilogram of rice would fill fifty baths; to produce the same weight in beef is around three hundred baths, mostly for growing feed for the animals (Foxwood & Green 2004).

However, a reduction in meat-eating is not the main concern for poor, small-scale farmers facing water shortages. As competition for water grows, it is these poor people who will be most threatened.

Tearfund partner River of Life is running a food security project in Zimbabwe called Operation Joseph, where farmers are encouraged to return to more traditional Conservation Farming principles (see Foxwood & Green 2004). One of the techniques is to make small holes in the topsoil instead of ploughing; rainwater collects in these. The ground around the holes is covered with organic material, such as plant debris, which stops the water evaporating, the top soil being washed away, and provides nutrients as it decomposes. Despite political uncertainties in Zimbabwe, it seems the project has been successful in providing many farmers previously facing hunger with sustainable food production.

Pollution

Even when there is enough water in the right place, it may be polluted and unfit for most domestic purposes. The World Water Assessment Programme estimates that 50% of the populations of developing countries are exposed to polluted water from industrial, municipal or agricultural sources. Two million tons of industrial wastes and chemicals, agricultural pesticides and fertilizers are disposed of every day into watercourses (UN/WWAP 2003).

Many developing countries are particularly affected because they lack the institutional and structural arrangements to deal with waste properly:

> India's rivers, especially the smaller ones, have all turned into toxic streams. And even the big ones such as the Ganges are far from pure. The assault on India's rivers – from population growth, agricultural modernization, urbanization and industrialization – is enormous and growing by the day . . . Most Indian cities get a large part of their drinking water from rivers. This entire life stands to be threatened.
> (Centre for Science and Environment 1999)

Poor people are especially vulnerable, as their whole livelihood may depend on water resources.

Climate change

Scientists predict that global climate change will increase the intensity of existing water problems. According to the Intergovernmental Panel on Climate Change (see Chapter 3), changes to the climate in Africa through the alteration of spatial and temporal patterns in temperature, rainfall, solar radiation and wind patterns will increase desertification and drought, hence having a direct impact on the ability of poor communities to grow food.

In Asia, climate change and variability will exacerbate the vulnerability of local communities to heat and water stresses and to extreme climate events like typhoons, cyclones, droughts and floods. Increased rainfall intensity, particularly during the summer monsoon, will increase flooding danger in temperate and tropical Asia. Sea-level rise will inundate large areas. In arid and semi-arid Asia, there is the likelihood of drier conditions during the summer, leading to more severe droughts. Freshwater availability will be highly vulnerable to anticipated climate change in Asia. Again, food insecurity is a primary concern (Roach 2005).

In Latin America, climate change will bring increased risk of floods and droughts in many different regions, associated with El Niño events. (El Niño is responsible for a large part of the climate variability in Latin America.) Population growth and unsustainable development of water-consuming activities will aggravate the effects of climate change on the hydrological cycle, with associated consequences for rainfall distribution, intensity and timing, surface runoff and underground water resources. In parts of Mexico and Latin America, climate change will mean about 70% of the population will be living in areas with low water supply as soon as the first quarter of the twenty-first century. Dry seasons are expected to become longer and more intense in many parts of Latin America. Predicted increases in temperature will reduce crop yields (Roach 2005).

Solutions

Managing resources like water to cope with all these challenges and demands is a major challenge for so-called 'developed countries', but it is quite simply not a priority for the governments of poorer countries, despite numerous treaties and international conferences. While some developing countries like South Africa and Brazil may have impressive-sounding national policies in place, the reality is that they do not have enough people with the skills and resources to implement them.

The good news is that there is increasing consensus among hydrologists, environmentalists and development workers on how we should manage our water resources. The consensus is a framework with the uninspiring title of 'integrated water resource management' (IWRM). It is a common-sense approach, making it difficult to understand why the management of water resources was ever done differently. The traditional approach, and the one still used by the majority of countries, is to look at the use of water resources on a sector-by-sector approach. Thus a Ministry of Agriculture considers the water needs for food production without consideration of what the Ministry of Environment may consider essential for wildlife and healthy ecosystems or what the Ministry of Local Government may be planning with regard to increasing access to drinking water in rural communities.

The IWRM model takes into account all the different users of water (industry, ecosystems, domestic, agriculture) in a water 'catchment' or 'basin'. These are the landscape units within which all water is gathered and made available for use. IWRM also seeks to coordinate the management of land, water (groundwater and surface water) and other environmental resources.

IWRM plans should facilitate and encourage traditional and local water management techniques, particularly in regard to agriculture. National frameworks like IWRM plans are needed, but their implementation has to be at the lowest level possible so that poor communities and other stakeholders are involved in decisions that are often a matter of life and death for them. Tearfund partner EFICOR in India argues that 'despite ample and credible evidence of the value of traditional methods (e.g. rainwater harvesting) employed to obtain and conserve water within river basins, they continue to be marginalized and trivialized. It is time to mainstream these locally rooted strategies by incorporating them into policies and budgets at all levels' (Foxwood & Green 2004: 8).

Water catchments do not respect political boundaries and may spread over several different countries. This makes it essential for national water resource management plans to involve upstream and downstream countries and for them to work together for regional water resource management agreements. The Nile Basin Initiative, for example, involves around ten countries. While many talk of wars over water, it may be more helpful to take a glass-half-full approach and consider ways our common dependence on water could spur countries and peoples to cooperate rather than conflict.

The international community agreed at the World Summit on Sustainable Development in 2002 that every country would 'develop integrated water resource management and water efficiency plans by 2005' (UN Department of Economic and Social Affairs 2004). Rich countries promised to support poor countries to achieve this ambitious target. This deadline has now passed with very little notice or concern from governments or global institutions. There is not even a body officially charged with monitoring progress. The most recent data are 'an informal' study in 2003 by the Global Water Partnership, a global organization specializing in water resource management. At that time, only 10 or 11 of 108 countries surveyed had 'made good progress', 50% had taken 'some steps' and 40% were still at the initial stage (UNESCO 2006: 72).

This lack of progress combined with growing water scarcity, pollution and climate change makes the need for integrated water and land management extremely urgent. A massive effort is urgently needed to support developing countries to manage the resource for the people who depend on it now and in generations to come.

People

Most people without access to safe water for domestic uses (drinking, washing and cooking) are short not because of a lack of water, but because governments have failed to provide it for them. Compared to the huge amounts needed for agriculture, the amount of water needed for basic human needs is relatively small: just fifteen litres per day.

Some years ago, I visited one of Tearfund's partners in south-west Uganda, the Kigezi Diocese Water and Sanitation Programme in Kabale District. Kabale is hilly, relatively wet, heavily populated and poor. I was taken to a hilltop community called Kagarama. The nearest safe supply of water was at the bottom of the hill, a two- to three-hour trip there and back. Most people chose to use water from a small pond just outside the village because it was much more convenient. But it was little more than a stagnant puddle: animals drank from it and churned up mud; women washed the family's clothes in it; everyone took water for drinking and cooking. The pond was a breeding ground for disease and mosquitoes, a source of intestinal worms, diarrhoea and malaria. Just looking at it and smelling it was horrendous; I found it difficult to imagine how desperate you would have to be to drink it. The women of Kagarama had a difficult decision: use water from this source or make the long journey to the bottom of the hill twice a day.

Meeting the Millennium Development Goals

There are over a billion people like these women, without access to safe water. Also, 2.6 billion live without access to adequate sanitation (WHO/UNICEF 2004). In the year 2000, world leaders committed themselves to the Millennium Development Goals (MDGs): to halve world poverty by 2015. The MDGs include a target on water: to halve the proportion of people without access to safe drinking water by 2015. In 2002, the World Summit on Sustainable Development added a further target: to halve by the same date the proportion of people without access to basic sanitation.

If the world is to meet these targets, every day 260,000 people will have to gain access to safe water and 370,000 to basic sanitation (WHO/UNICEF 2004). In terms of global averages, the world is on track to meet the MDG for water, but way off to meet the sanitation goal (WaterAid 2005). Without a dramatic improvement in provision, nearly 2.4 billion people will still be without adequate sanitation in 2015 – almost as many as today.

Less than half the rural population of Africa has access to safe water. Unless something changes dramatically the water target will not be met until 2050 and it will be 2100 at the earliest before the sanitation target is achieved. An estimated 133 million African children will die if the water and sanitation targets are not met on their continent, lives that otherwise could have been saved (WHO/UNICEF 2000).

Of the 2.6 billion people lacking sanitation, 80% live in rural areas, half of them in India and China (WHO/UNICEF 2000). Incredibly, there are more people in India who have access to cable TV than to toilets. Although Asia has a higher proportion than Africa with access to water, it has a much larger population than any other continent; as a result, the numbers in need in Asia are the largest.

High population growth in the developing world combined with rapid urbanization, often into 'informal settlements', means that filling current gaps in water provision and sanitation services is not enough, particularly in Africa. Between 1990 and 1994 people with access to municipal supplies actually *decreased* from 82% to 64%. Just to keep up with population growth in urban areas up to 2015 means an estimated 913 million additional people will need access to water supply and 834 million to sanitation (WHO/UNICEF 2000).

Women

Access to water is a top priority for poor people, especially women (DFID 2004). Women and girls in Africa and Asia have to travel an average of six kilometres to collect water, and carry about twenty kilograms of water. This is exhausting and often dangerous. Furthermore, time spent walking to and from water points is often time spent not attending school. Female illiteracy in particular will persist as long as there is inadequate access to water. Illness from poor sanitation and dirty water will also prevent children going to school. A UNICEF study in Nigeria found that access to water and sanitation increased the enrolment in school by 20% (UNICEF n.d.b).

In Kigezi, I was taken to many communities where the diocesan staff had worked with the people to provide safe access to water and sanitation, and improve hygiene practices. The schemes varied according to the geographical and hydrological situation. Gravity-flow schemes are the most straightforward, where water comes from a protected spring and the flow is maintained entirely by gravity via one or more service reservoirs and a piped distribution system to public tap-stands. A spring source can be protected either to supply a gravity scheme or just to provide a continuously running outlet, and allow a bucket or container to be placed below it. Sometimes rainwater harvesting is the best option. This requires less technical expertise, although it is still a demanding project. In these cases, the Diocese trains women's groups to build storage tanks for each house and install guttering on their roofs that drains to a downpipe and discharges into a storage tank.

The women in these communities testified to the many positive ways the project had improved the quality of their lives and empowered them economically and socially by reduction in disease and child deaths. One women's group I visited described their delight in clambering over roofs to attach guttering. Other communities had offered to pay them to come and install rain-water harvesting structures on to their houses.

Working with women by involving them in decision-making, construction, and the operation and maintenance of the water point is vital to their success. Because water is usually the most pressing need, a water project will often be the first development project the women work on together. This inspires them as well as freeing them to move on to addressing other issues such as food security.

Disease

According to UNICEF, lack of safe water and sanitation is the world's single largest cause of illness. Water-related diseases kill more than five million people every year, both through water providing the medium by which disease is transmitted and as the habitat for disease-transmitting insects. Half the population in the developing world suffer from one or more of the main diseases associated with poor water and sanitation: diarrhoea, ascaris, dracunculiasis (guinea worm), hookworm, schistosomiasis (bilharzia or snail fever) and trachoma.

The statistics for diarrhoea are shocking: 'about 4 billion cases of diarrhoea per year cause 1.8 million deaths, over 90% of them (1.6 million) among children under five. Repeated episodes of diarrhoeal disease makes children more vulnerable to other diseases and malnutrition' (http://rehydrate.org/about/index.html). Diarrhoea is the third-biggest child killer in Africa, and accounts for 701,000 child deaths out of 4.4 million on the continent every year (UNICEF n.d.a). A baby born in sub-Saharan Africa is five hundred times more likely to die from diarrhoeal disease than one born in the developed world. Improving people's access to water reduces cases of diarrhoea by 25% (Fewtrell et al. 2005).

The most common cause of preventable blindness is trachoma: some six million people worldwide have lost their sight from this disease, yet 'there is sufficient scientific evidence to support the notion that with improved hygiene and access to water and sanitation trachoma will disappear . . . as it has from Europe and North America' (UNESCO 2006: 229).

The economic impact
Poor health caused by water-related diseases has a terrible effect on national economies and poor people's livelihoods. Seventy-three million working days are lost every year in India alone from waterborne diseases. A cholera outbreak in Peru in the early 1990s cost the economy US$1 billion in just ten weeks in lost tourism and agricultural exports. Women in rural areas are responsible for half the world's food production, and produce between 60 and 80% of food in most developing countries. Yet having to collect water drastically cuts the time they can spend on income-generating activities such as agriculture.

People living in slums often have to buy water at extortionate prices from vendors because they have no access to a piped network. In Karachi, Pakistan, poor people living in areas without sanitation or hygiene education spend six times more on basic medical care than those in areas with basic sanitation and hygiene training (Hutton & Haller 2004). Spending large amounts of money on water means other important services, such as education and healthcare, are neglected, preventing people from climbing out of poverty.

Paradoxically, the cost of *not* providing safe water and adequate sanitation in developing countries is higher than the cost of piping in water and building latrines. The World Health Organization has calculated that failure to invest in water, sanitation and work towards the MDG target is costing developing countries US$84 billion per year in health and other expenses, while the time saved by having more convenient drinking water and sanitation services would amount to twenty billion working days a year, giving a payback in productivity of about US$63 billion a year (Hutton & Haller 2004).

Sanitation and hygiene

Inadequate sanitation and poor hygiene get far less attention than lack of access to safe water, but are a much bigger challenge, especially for women. There is a lack of understanding of the links between sanitation, hygiene and poor health, even though the number of people who do not have access to sanitation is more than double those without access to water. Hygiene education and promoting hand-washing reduces cases of diarrhoea by 45%. Improving people's access to safe water and better hygiene can cut the incidence of trachoma by more than 25% (WHO 2004). One problem is that there is often not a strong demand for improved sanitation: open defecation is ingrained in people's behaviour in Asian countries such as India and Bangladesh. Changing such behaviour is very difficult, especially when cultural and religious norms are attached and there is little demand for change. But without improved hygiene behaviour and basic sanitation, the health impacts of a safe water supply will not be realized. If people defecate in the open, faeces can easily contaminate food and water supplies.

Poor access to sanitation impacts women disproportionately. They often face strict cultural taboos that force them to walk for miles or wait until after dark to relieve themselves. Understandably, this is not an issue women find easy to talk about or request. In my own travels to visit Tearfund's partners, it has rarely been appropriate to talk to women about the impact of poor sanitation on their lives. I can sympathize with that: I can't imagine opening my home to a complete stranger and being prepared to tell them when and where I went to the toilet!

However, in one visit to a village called Gawada in southern Ethiopia, I spoke to a mother and teacher called Brahani who felt happy to discuss the water *and* sanitation aspects of the Kale Heywet Church's project. She explained that before the water and sanitation programme came to the village, the inhabitants had to use dirty water from an unprotected spring. Now they have bio-sand filters in each home that purify the water by removing disease-causing particles. It is low-cost and simple technology. Brahani told me, 'I spend half the day at school and the remaining time in the house cooking and looking after the children, and trying to increase our income.' Having the filter has improved the quality of her life because it provides clean water and saves time. She has also benefited from the sanitation aspect of the project: 'Because of the disease, it was difficult before, especially with five children! Women were ashamed to defecate during the day time, but for men it was no problem: they could go whenever they wanted. We had to wait until it was dark and I was afraid of being attacked by wild animals or drunkards.'

The team of community workers worked with the people to show them the need for adequate sanitation and good hygiene practices. They showed the people how to construct a pit-latrine. Brahani described life in the village as good now, as the disease has decreased, in particular the incidence of diarrhoea that used to cause many deaths. She testified to the success of the project, 'Sanitation is better here than other villages because we had education from the community workers about water-borne diseases, and so our sanitation and hygiene has improved. We have learnt how to keep the house and environment clean . . . and we have discussed community problems. We have a pit-latrine that works well; it was installed three years ago and we have one in every house.'

There tends to be a higher demand for sanitation and sewerage in urban areas because of the close-quarters living conditions. In Ethiopia, I visited a WaterAid-supported project in the slums of Addis Ababa and spoke to Frehiwot, who was studying at college and about to go on to a diploma programme. She recalled that before a local non-governmental organization had installed the latrines the slum dwellers had no toilets. Those who had jobs defecated at work. 'I was fortunate because I could go when I was at school,' she told me. Those who weren't so fortunate had to walk to an open field or use a very small patch of wasteland next to where the toilets now stand. The impact on the community was terrible: 'We had diseases like typhoid and the children especially had many diseases. Some women had to pay to use the toilet because they were too scared to go out at night to the field.' Eating was not a pleasurable experience because 'the women would be thinking where will we be able to go to the toilet? We were really angry because we had no money to build a latrine, so we complained to the government. Now we are happy that we have the latrines.' The result was a significant reduction in disease. There was still a sewerage problem: for twelve years people had thrown their waste into an open sewer and blocked it. At the time of my visit no-one had done anything about this.

Solutions

So what needs to be done to address these widespread problems? There are some generally applicable principles, such as the need to work with and empower women, and the need for technological solutions to be appropriate. There are political and financial frameworks that have to be put in place to support locally driven solutions. Governments in developing countries need to take on the responsibility of providing their citizens with basic services. As a first step they need to make a political commitment at the highest level to meeting the MDG targets, and this commitment has to be costed and translated into realistic water and sanitation strategies and plans. However, even these actions are beyond the capacities of many governments. Responsibilities for water, sanitation and hygiene tend to be shared between several ministries, making consensus-building and coordination a major challenge. Recruiting enough well-qualified civil servants to develop the plans can be very difficult when salaries are   low. Developed nations must be ready to give support to developing countries when they make a political commitment to the MDGs, and must also improve governance, including help with finance and other necessities.

Unfortunately, this has not happened in many cases. The intention behind the MDGs and the Millennium Declaration was to signify an internationally shared determination to poverty alleviation. Developing countries agreed to prioritize poverty reduction, and developed countries to address global inequalities in aid, trade and debt that have helped create and perpetuate poverty. Six years later, developed countries' response to the water and sanitation crisis has been woefully inadequate. At the time of writing, aid from rich countries has in fact been declining since 1997 (Foxwood & Green 2004). The need for more spending on sanitation in particular is pressing. The World Health Organization has estimated that meeting the MDG for sanitation will absorb 84% of the total additional funding needed to hit both water and sanitation targets. Although more than twice as many people lack access to basic sanitation than to safe water in Africa, sanitation attracts only one-eighth of the funding that water gets (WHO/UNICEF 2000).

Developed countries should give equal priority in their aid to all the basic services: health, education, water and sanitation. But this is not the case: they give much more to education than to water and sanitation. In 2004, spending on education amounted to 9.7% of overall aid, compared with 4.9% on health and slightly more on water and sanitation. Although roughly the same amount of aid is given to health as to water and sanitation, much of the water and sanitation aid is in the form of loans rather than grants, pushing developing countries into debt just for providing this basic service. Between 2000 and 2004, the average total of grants each year for health was US$1.54 billion, more than double the US$0.76 billion provided to water and sanitation projects; loans for the former totalled US$0.58 billion, for the latter US$1.12 billion (Tearfund 2006a).

Access to water is a top priority for poor people: water, sanitation and hygiene are major factors in better health for poor people and for female school attendance. These issues have been neglected for too long. It is essential that water, sanitation and hygiene get a just share of the increases in aid and debt relief agreed in 2005. Only then will the developed countries truly fulfil the promises they made at the Millennium Summit (the UN meeting held in 2000, where world leaders agreed the Millennium Development Goals).

As far as the developing countries are concerned, much needs to be done: to support civil society (including the church), to empower poor people to demand better water and sanitation services, and to encourage good governance, holding governments to account for promises made.

The challenges of the water crisis in terms of resource management, food production and lack of access to water and sanitation are enormous and the answers are complex. It is easy to be daunted by depressing statistics and the immensity of the task, yet there are many inspiring and incredible stories of Christian organizations demonstrating the glory of God through practical service and through challenging unjust structures and oppressive powers.

Let us press on and play our part in helping the poor of the developing world gain and retain access to safe drinking water, basic sanitation and enough water for sustainable food production.

© Joanne Green, 2007

9. SUSTAINABILITY, RESOURCES AND WASTE

David Stafford and John Bryant

David Stafford is Managing Director of Enviro-Control Ltd, a Monmouth, UK, company specializing in developing 'waste to energy' products worldwide. He is a Visiting Professor at West Virginia State University and author of several books on waste treatment. He acts as a consultant to governments and international companies on issues relating to carbon emissions and bio-remediation.

John Bryant was Professor of Biological Sciences at the University of Exeter from 1985 to 2002 and is now Professor Emeritus; he is Visiting Professor of Molecular Biology at West Virginia State University. He is a Fellow of the Wessex Institute of Technology, Chairman of the Higher Education Academy's special interest group on Teaching Ethics to Bioscience Students and a former President of the Society for Experimental Biology. John Bryant is a co-author of Bioethics for Scientists *(John Wiley & Sons, 2002), of* Life in our Hands *(IVP, 2004) and* Introduction to Bioethics *(John Wiley & Sons, 2005). He was Chairman of Christians in Science 2001–7.*

How different is the world from the way it is meant to be?

One of the themes that runs throughout Scripture is that the universe and everything in it is God's: God is the creator; the universe in all its complexity and magnificence is his creation. He cares for and about his creation and 'has not left himself without testimony: He has shown kindness by giving you rain from heaven and crops in their seasons; he provides you with plenty of food and fills your hearts with joy' (Acts 14:17).

Daniel is a good role model for us. He knew a life of turmoil, but acknowledged God as the sustainer of his life and environment and continued to give honour to God and trust in his providence despite all that happened. He also believed God would do something different in the future: bring in a kingdom that will never be destroyed (Dan. 2:44). In Daniel's diary we see several visions, one of which is a Man standing over the river of history, in whose hands are our political and environmental world. We need a vision like this to encourage us to look after the present world and look forward to a new world.

We need this, because instead of caring for the world, we have exploited its resources with little acknowledgment that they may be finite; and in the process have severely damaged the earth itself. As biologist-priest David de Pomerai has put it:

> Entire ecosystems have been devastated in the name of Western progress, entailing forest destruction, decimation of dominant animals (such as bison) and massacres of indigenous peoples. More recently, we have added industrial pollution and intensive agriculture to the growing degradation . . . The original sense of responsible stewardship implicit in the Hebrew word for 'dominion' (as in Gen. 1:28) has become lost beneath a welter of profiteering and greed. (De Pomerai 2002: 88)

At the same time, the idea of a Creator and the associated sense of stewardship and responsibility have largely disappeared.[1] Pollution

---

1. The USA is an odd anomaly: there is a very widespread belief in God as creator and yet American society is particularly profligate in the use of the

has affected ground and air and water and this is the environment in which we live and breathe. So the key question is: *Are we as Christians interested in using the God-given resources of the earth wisely to the benefit of all, as we are charged by the two 'great commandments' to love God and to love our neighbour?*

Energy, waste and climate change

There are now a decreasing number of dissentients that human-mediated climate change will lead to drier semi-desert regions, more storms in temperate climes, glacier melts, a significant sea-level rise, and a movement towards the temperate regions of tropical diseases such as malaria (Smil 1999, 2001; Haines et al. 2006). We do not yet know whether the increase in carbon dioxide concentration in the atmosphere will stimulate plant growth in the sea and in tropical rainforests, but we are only too aware that the latter are diminishing by an area of about the size of Wales per year. And if the glaciers melt and the ice caps shrink, this will increase the amount of cold water in the oceans and could reduce the flow of the Gulf Stream, and thus change the climate of western Europe very quickly. But even worse, and the scariest prediction of all, is that an increase in sea temperatures of only a few degrees will lead to the release of methane hydrates from the bottom of the oceans. The atmosphere would be filled with methane that will spontaneously combust, producing a worldwide fire; this could happen within as little as ten years at the current rate of warming.

It is also clear that the production and treatment of wastes generated by human activities affect directly both greenhouse gas emissions (and thus global warming) and other aspects of global pollution. Waste treatment is thus a very pressing problem as six billion people use more and more of the earth's resources and generate more and more waste. Further, as major countries such as

---

earth's resources (Southgate 2002; Bryant, Baggott la Velle & Searle 2005; Gore 2006) (although there are signs of positive change in that nation).

China and India become more affluent, this problem will increase dramatically, accompanied by increased distortion of natural processes (Bryant, Baggott la Velle & Searle 2005). A good example of the latter is the Haber-Bosch process for fixing atmospheric nitrogen, which is now the single largest contributor to the nitrogen (N) cycle. The effect of this inorganic nitrogen on both human health and biodiversity is a cause of some concern. Humans alter the N-cycle more than either the carbon or sulphur cycles (Smil 2001), but interference in the sulphur cycle may also be a problem: human activity releases about eighty tonnes of sulphur per year from burning fossil fuels, although this pales into insignificance when compared to the thousands of tonnes emitted by volcanic eruptions.

We also have to take into account the wide range of organic wastes produced by corporate, industrial, municipal, agricultural and individual activities. If we use aerobic means to treat these wastes, be it incineration, gasification or biological aerobic systems, we produce an enormous amount of carbon dioxide as well as contributing adversely to public health (Stafford, West & White 1993). Intensive farming, while providing cheap food for many, raises particular problems. An average pig farm produces up to a hundred tonnes per day of highly polluting waste, while some large cattle farms produce thousands of tonnes every day. These may have to be trucked hundreds of miles to be disposed of remotely and from where methane and carbon dioxide emanate. Methane is twenty-three times more potent as a greenhouse gas than carbon dioxide weight for weight. This is truly a serious problem.

All this seems very far removed from the character of God and the magnificence of his creation:

> But ask the animals, and they will teach you,
>   or the birds of the air, and they will tell you;
> or speak to the earth, and it will teach you,
>   or let the fish of the sea inform you.
> Which of all these does not know
>   that the hand of the LORD has done this?
> (Job 12:7–9)

What are the environmental issues?

Studies into the relationships between life forms and the rest of the world accelerated in the nineteenth century and the term *biosphere* was coined at that time. Such questions as 'What is the importance of the organic world in the general scheme of chemical reactions on Earth?' began to be asked. These questions have assumed a much greater urgency as we increasingly realize that the activity of humans has very dramatic effects on that general scheme. Global issues giving cause for serious concern are as follows:

1. We are returning to the atmosphere over a century or so concentrated organic carbon that was stored over a period of millions of years. Looking at the carbon dioxide concentration over the last 400,000 years or so, we see it reaching levels never seen before in that time scale. Similarly, atmospheric methane levels are higher than at any time over the last several thousand years. Global climate change driven by increases in greenhouse gases is leading to an increasing rate of planetary warming.
2. Excessive application of and poor disposal of organic and inorganic nitrogen compounds contributes further to climate change and other global problems.
3. Conversion of huge biomass resources for our own use plus extensive deforestation are causing an unprecedented loss in biodiversity. Deforestation is also causing water pollution, especially in developing countries with little or no effluent treatment systems. In respect of the loss of biodiversity, extinctions are occurring at least fifty to a hundred times faster than the background rate over geological time and are predicted to occur at a thousand times or more than the background rate by 2020 (Lawton & May 1995; United Nations Environmental Programme 1995; IUCN 2006). Indeed, as so poignantly described by Christian biologist John Spicer, it is certain that many species are becoming extinct before they have been discovered, and thus, although they coexisted with humankind, humankind will never know them (Spicer 2006).

4. Atmospheric and water contamination with chemicals derived from industry.
5. Substantial seasonal weakening of the ozone layer.

These problems are interconnected. The most potent greenhouse gases are carbon dioxide, methane and nitrous oxide. They create layers in the upper atmosphere that capture heat and radiate it back to Earth. Such chemicals as ammonia, organic sulphur compounds, sulphur dioxide and nitrogen organic compounds are directly affecting plant animal and human life (West et al. 1995). Most of the particulate pollutants in the atmosphere are present in small amounts (a few parts per million), but sufficient to induce serious diseases such as asthma, cancer, heart disease and renal failure. DDT has been illegal in developed countries since 1972, but aromatic and chlorinated hydrocarbons are still being produced and are related to increases in leukaemia and respiratory disease (Stafford, West & White 1993). Furthermore, farms may rival industry in pollution production. One cattle farm in California produces more particulate volatile organics than all the cars in Los Angeles put together, because car emissions have been controlled, whereas cattle have not. Sulphur emissions from human activity globally rose from five million tonnes per year in 1900 to eighty million tonnes per year in 2000 (Smil 2003). While in the US and Europe such atmospheric emissions have declined, in the Far East, especially China, sulphur dioxide from fossil fuel combustion accounts for at least 75% of global emissions. China now burns 25% more coal than the USA (Smil 2003) and with less efficient combustion and dirtier processes.[2]

We have an increasing knowledge of how individual organisms and particular ecosystems adapt to changing conditions. However, we lack detailed knowledge of global interactions and many of our predictions are based on limited empirical observations plus

---

2. Recent visitors to China have noted that attitudes there are changing, perhaps partly because the country will be 'on show' during the 2008 Olympic Games. Thus in some cities there are electric and dual-fuel taxis and electric motor cycles.

computer-generated models that may well be flawed. Nevertheless, the lack of *detailed* predictions does not obscure the overall picture.

What can be done?

The scale of the problem of waste is vividly encapsulated by a seven-metre-high statue of a robotic humanoid weighing 3.3 tonnes made from all the electronic and electrical equipment used and discarded by the average inhabitant of the UK in a lifetime (see figure on next page). It was commissioned by the Royal Society of Arts and designed by Paul Bonomini (see http://www.weeeman.org/index.html) and given the name WEEE Man in acknowledgment of the European Union's Waste Electrical and Electronic Equipment Directive. Quite apart from the amount of material making up the statue, we should take into account also the energy used in both manufacturing and running the equipment. When we multiply all this from one individual to the many millions living at similar or greater levels of affluence and when we extend our thinking to all the other resources used by the average inhabitant of a developed Western society, we begin to have some appreciation of the vastness of the problem (see also Southgate 2002; Bryant, Baggott la Velle & Searle 2005).

Faced with such data, it is very easy to fall into a totally negative frame of mind, but we should note that actually, change is possible. Who could have predicted in 1986 that the Berlin Wall would fall, and with it the command economies of the eastern bloc? The countries of Eastern Europe then became subject to Western pollution laws, which, coupled with changing employment patterns, have led to a great reduction in the emission of atmospheric pollutants. Another positive example is the universal banning of chlorofluorocarbons from refrigerators, enabling the ozone layer to begin recovering. Reversing the trend of global climate change will not be so easy, but that is no reason for not attempting it (Pacala & Socolow 2004).

A starting point must be to regain a strong sense of stewardship, acknowledging that the world is not our own. Further, even

Figure: The RSA WEEE Man, installed at the Eden Project, Cornwall.
Photograph by Nick Gregory. © RSA.

though as Christians we recognize stewardship as a responsibility
to God, we have argued elsewhere that stewardship is an equally
valid concept in the secular world and can be applied as a guiding
principle by those who do not share our faith (Bryant, Baggott la
Velle & Searle 2005). It is also clear that stewardship should
embody a concern for our fellow human beings wherever they are,
and this concern for our neighbour should be trans-generational.

This idea of responsibility to future generations has been part of secular thinking on environmental issues for some time (e.g. Potter 1971) and is now being more widely adopted in Christian thinking (e.g. Reiss 2002; Bryant & Searle 2004). Indeed, as Hay indicates (Chapter 6), an attitude of stewardship in use of the earth's resources should lead us to ask what sort of world we are leaving for our great-grandchildren (see also Spicer 2006).

So, whether based in a Judeo-Christian or a secular context, how can the principle of stewardship be worked out? We suggest that the *three Rs* of resource use and waste management are applicable here:

- *Restraint*: taking seriously the fact that many resources are finite and linking to a move to renewable sources. It will mean striving for environmental integrity and attempting to reject all profligate use.
- *Re-use*: reversing the 'throwaway' attitudes that permeate our culture.
- *Recycle*: to bring back into use materials and energy locked up in waste material of all sorts.

The responsibilities for acting on these three Rs lie at all levels: individuals, large and small organizations, industry, local, national and international governments and global agencies. At each of these levels it is possible to identify appropriate actions that have some effect on the situation. For example, we are capable of dramatically reducing our energy consumption. The mean energy use in western Europe is 150 gigajoules per head per year; that of the USA is 350 gigajoules per head per year. If China or India followed our example, we would have dramatic and serious increases in pollution and carbon outputs. However, it has been shown that about one-third reduction of the energy enjoyed in the UK would not reduce our quality of life, life span or other measurements of well-being (Smil 2003; see also Chapter 5). The question is how this is possible.

Practical action

Many companies are now embracing corporate governance protocols for resource use and the treatment of industrial wastes, with members and shareholders asking questions about the transparency of the organization in ecological or environmental issues and how accountable its officers are to shareholders or the public. Key issues are the training and competence of employees to understand the importance of environmental issues and the application of knowledge to help determine the way forward. We know of a Marks & Spencer warehouse where lorry routes are continually monitored and adjusted to maximize efficiency and where the fuel consumption of each truck and the energy budget of the whole warehouse are checked weekly. These activities are driven by a particular warehouse manager who is concerned about the environment. Obviously, the incorporation of such policies right across the company's delivery network could both reduce carbon pollution and save the company money. In addition, the site we describe has been planted with trees and a small area of wetland has been kept as a reserve. There is no reason why similar approaches should not be adopted by other companies and organizations.

In respect of waste and effluents, alternatives exist for the treatment of waste organic compounds, using anaerobic systems linked to energy generation and thereby reducing fossil fuel use (Stafford 1983). The aromatic compounds produced by industry can now be treated using anaerobic bacteria without need for external energy sources. The disposal of analgesics and steroids commonly used to treat arthritic conditions is polluting sewage and rivers (where they are related to sex-reversal of some fish); again newer bacterial systems can be developed to deal with this.

However, human greed may interfere with such approaches. When companies incorporate sustainable technologies and processes and try to reduce environmental impacts, shareholders may object if this seems to reduce profit margins. Nevertheless, if properly handled, the 'greening' of a company can improve both turnover and the bottom line, not least because a growing part of the population is seeking ecofriendly products. In the USA, a large bank is spending about $1 billion in building ecofriendly buildings so that little or no external energy input is needed for running the buildings. Japan is leading the introduction of hybrid cars that can provide a highly efficient use of fossil fuels. The advent of bio-diesel highlights the *growing* of fuel for existing diesel engines. Is the switch from petrol to diesel-engine cars thus increasing fuel use efficiency and saving money, something all individuals and organizations should consider? Several of the larger fuel and engineering companies are now embracing green technologies and seeing a market opportunity as well. In the USA, 'green' products are being increasingly sought by consumers; the current 'hike' in oil prices will presumably increase this trend.

Although such signs are encouraging, there is a real danger of a worsening of environmental quality if, as predicted by some models, the world's population nearly doubles.[3] Increases in greenhouse gas emissions, water and air pollution will carry on apace. Indeed, Frances Cairncross, President of the British Association for the Advancement of Science for 2005–6 suggested in her presidential address (Cairncross 2006; see also Stanhope & Crawford 2006) that we need to accept that global climate change is happening and work to ameliorate its effects. That does not mean we should give up trying to halt or reverse the trend but that we should also do something now to help those who are most vulnerable and look for ways of preserving biodiversity. The best aim must be to reverse climate change, but this is certainly not easy: human complacency and the self-centredness of human nature get in the way. Even commentators with no religious faith recognize this problem; for Paul Ehrlich 'our challenge is to learn to deal with both nature and human nature' (Smil 2003: 113).

Thus it is incumbent on us to

- determine what we can do as individual stewards;
- join our efforts with those of others in wider society;
- make wider society aware of what can be done;
- where possible, inform, lobby and influence community leaders and policy-makers, including representatives of local and national government.

---

3. Although it should be noted that in late 2006 some commentators were suggesting that the growth in the human population of the earth is slowing significantly.

While acting on our own may seem discouraging and, indeed, ineffective, we can be encouraged that individuals and groups of individuals can make a difference. Recent publications by the Department for International Development (Wroe & Doney 2004) and by Tearfund (2006b) encourage us that we can all do something worthwhile. For example, in a different context, the publication by the UK Government of a Bill that will make it illegal to possess or even view violent pornography resulted from a campaign initiated by one woman whose daughter had been killed. Relevant to the theme of this book is the very welcome growth of the Christian 'creation care' movement in the USA. Although there have been exceptions (such as those who spearheaded the 'What would Jesus drive?' movement), much of the American evangelical Christian community has hitherto been sceptical about global climate change, but this has changed due to a large extent to the tireless work of Sir John Houghton (Houghton & Henderson 2006), one of the authors of this volume, in lobbying and informing Christian leaders in the USA. Indeed, one of those leaders, Rich Cizik, describes hearing Houghton speak on climate change as like having another conversion experience (reported on the website of the John Ray Initiative: http://www.jri.org.uk).

Returning again to what can be done, people's circumstances make them able to consider particular courses of action differently. In rural areas of the UK and throughout much of the USA, for example, there is little or no public transport and this will affect decisions about cars. Our own health will also influence our choices in transport and domestic energy usage. Nevertheless, we suggest some pointers:

- *Personal transport.* Do we need the car(s) we own? Work out the cash value of the cars in our church car parks. Do we need them all? Could we pool our cars or set up a car-pooling system. Is our car fuel-efficient? What fuel does it run on? Do we use our cars for journeys where walking or cycling would be more appropriate?
- *Public transport.* Can we use it more often instead of using our car? Where public transport is less than adequate, will we lobby the relevant authorities to improve it? Are we willing to help pay, from our national or local taxes, for improvements in public transport?

- *Domestic energy use.*[4] How warm do we keep our homes? Even a one-degree reduction in thermostat setting will save significant amounts of energy. For how many hours a day do we heat our homes or our hot water supply? Do we use lights unnecessarily? Can we switch to low-energy light bulbs? Do we leave TVs, DVD players and so forth on standby?
- *Domestic energy generation.* Are we prepared to pay for domestic systems that use renewable energy sources? Such systems include solar panels, photovoltaic cells and mini-turbines. Are we prepared to lobby local planning officers to permit such technologies in conservation areas?
- *The throwaway society.* The situation portrayed by the RSA WEEE man statue should certainly make us think. Can we reduce the rate at which we replace our domestic goods and motor vehicles? Should we lobby manufacturers to make equipment both more durable and easier to repair? Can we reverse a situation in which it is often easier and cheaper to buy new than to repair existing goods?
- *Food.* Are we concerned about 'food miles'? Do we try to buy, where appropriate, locally sourced foods and, if circumstances permit, grow some of our own? In the UK, the use of heavy goods vehicles (HGVs) to transport food doubled between 1974 and 2002. The cost to the environment of transport by HGVs is four times greater than if the same load were transported by rail. Since autumn 2005, the supermarket chain Sainsbury's has been transporting some goods by train (Van der Zee 2006).
- *Recycling.* Does our local authority have a workable recycling scheme? If not, should we lobby the local authority to do so? If

---

4. Reduction in domestic energy use can make a significant difference to national carbon dioxide output. It has been suggested that in a city of around a hundred thousand people it should be possible to make savings in energy consumption equivalent to the output of an average-sized power station (Alex Aylward, personal communication). Based on this a group of Christians in Exeter, UK, are working to achieve this in their city.

we have a garden, do we compost our waste plant material? Are we aware of and do we encourage research and development in waste management (e.g. that carried out at the Centre for Sustainable Wastes Management at the University of Northampton, under the direction of a Christian academic, Professor Paul Philips [http://www.northampton.ac.uk/research/centres])?

- *Land use.* Changes in family structure have led in the UK to a need for more housing units. Do we encourage the use of brownfield sites in order to conserve green space and hence biodiversity?
- *Carbon credits.* Are we aware of the carbon credits scheme? Can we lobby the government to apply the scheme in the implementation of waste-to-energy projects?
- *Environmental businesses.* Should those professionally involved with environmental and waste management issues be more active in encouraging water companies to use more efficient bacterial systems for sewage and industrial treatment and cut down on the use of electricity and costs? If appropriate, does our business embrace the technologies that permit more effective energy conservation, waste management and resource recycling?
- *General awareness.* Are we conscious of our own 'environmental footprint' and of ways of reducing it? Do we know about the impacts of new environmental technologies on economic growth, employment, competition and human well-being?

Our circumstances will determine what steps we can take and how active we can be, but in general we should all be looking for ways in which we can contribute to the solution of environmental problems rather than make them worse. Unfortunately, it is much easier to evaluate objectively the lifestyles of others. There is a significant challenge here for all of us to live authentic Christian lives.[5]

© David Stafford and John Bryant, 2007

---

5. We are grateful to Alex Aylward and Tim Miller for helpful discussion and to the RSA for permission to reproduce, free of charge, the photograph of the RSA WEEE Man.

10. CREATIVE HARMONY: ISAIAH'S VISION OF A SUSTAINABLE FUTURE

Margot R. Hodson

The Revd Margot Hodson is Chaplain of Jesus College, Oxford, and a director of the John Ray Initiative. She has degrees in geography and theology and a longstanding interest in issues of faith and environment. Her husband, Martin, is an environmental biologist, and both are active members of Sage, Oxford's Christian environmental group.

> Seek the LORD while he may be found;
>   call on him while he is near.
> Let the wicked forsake his way
>   and the evil man his thoughts.
> Let him turn to the LORD, and he will have mercy on him,
>   and to our God, for he will freely pardon.
> 'For my thoughts are not your thoughts,
>   neither are your ways my ways,' declares the LORD.
> 'As the heavens are higher than the earth,
>   so are my ways higher than your ways
>   and my thoughts than your thoughts.
> As the rain and the snow come down from heaven,
>   and do not return to it

without watering the earth
and making it bud and flourish,
    so that it yields seed for the sower and bread for the eater,
so is my word that goes out from my mouth:
    It will not return to me empty,
but will accomplish what I desire
    and achieve the purpose for which I sent it.
You will go out in joy
    and be led forth in peace;
the mountains and hills
    will burst into song before you,
and all the trees of the field
    will clap their hands.
Instead of the thornbush will grow the pine tree,
    and instead of briers the myrtle will grow.
This will be for the LORD's renown,
    for an everlasting sign,
    which will not be destroyed.'

                                        – Isaiah 55:6–13

Greg is a Philippine Christian from a community who live on the slopes of Mount Pinatubo. When the volcano erupted in 1991 (the largest eruption in the world for half a century), the village was destroyed, trees were turned to charcoal, and the top of the mountain was left as a vast crater that filled with water. Good forecasting had led to an evacuation before the eruption, and miraculously no lives were lost in their community. The villagers were rehoused on the edge of the nearest city in makeshift homes. But as rural people they could not make a living there: they were farmers and needed to have land to farm. So, after much discussion, they decided to return to the site of their village, despite its devastation, the fear that the large crater could overflow and flood them in the monsoon, and the uncertainty of living on an active volcano. Meanwhile, Greg had decided to take nine months out to train in sustainable farming methods at the Asian Rural Institute in Japan, a Christian centre training rural leaders in developing countries. After this, he intended to go back to his home region to help lead its resurrection, not simply in traditional Christian care but also in practical farming, using simple sustainable methods such as bio-mass energy generation.

Not far from Greg's village, the Philippine Faith Mission Inc. had set up a children's home for street children from Olongapo City. This also needed rebuilding after the eruption and sought sustainable solutions to their needs. Greg returned to the Pinatubo region and set up a farm project for the children's home. The Jezreel farm now provides food, income, training and employment for this growing Christian community. They have become self-sufficient in rice, and the organic, mixed-farming approach reduces the cost of external inputs, while maximizing the products of the farm.

Greg's story is a parable for a Christian response to the environmental, human and economic challenges we face in the twenty-first century. Committed to Christ, his call as a Christian led him to be a caring steward not only of the people of his community, but also of the unstable part of the earth where he had been placed. Despite the uncertainty of the future, the Christians of his region are committed to its resurrection. Rather than exploit it entirely for human gain, this group of people are seeking to farm it sustainably. As Greg and others in the Pinatubo region work to regenerate the fertile soils, allow the regrowth of the forests and re-establish their communities, we can begin to see a pattern of Christian living that seeks to find harmony between humanity, earth and the Creator.

Nature, people and God

Understanding how to balance human and environmental needs for present and future generations is an essential key to sustainable living, and this question is addressed in a number of places in the Hebrew Bible. The book of the prophet Isaiah in particular is rich in natural imagery and incisive in its social comment. It was written in the context of social and political turmoil, and the images of nature presented to us are related to human actions and to human interaction with God. Understanding how these relationships are portrayed enables us to uncover the underlying perception of the connection between God, humans and the rest of the material world. The world described is Canaan in the eighth to sixth centuries BC, which was the later Iron Age in the ancient Near East. It was a land of hills and valleys, streams, arid areas and mountainous woodland (Mathys 2004), making it very suitable for the mixed farming of the period; the area was significantly influenced by humans through the grazing of animals and terraced agriculture (Hepper 1992). Trees were prized and rain was seen as God's blessing. Farmers were dependent on the rains and there were always dangers from desertification from overploughing or overgrazing. Wilderness or desert was never far away and wild animals could intrude on domestic land. Despite all this, the wilderness was not seen negatively, but as the place where God dwelt and a place of potential fertility.

Social justice is a major theme in Isaiah, and practising injustice is linked to a consequent lack of fertility of the land (e.g. Isa. 5:8–10). There is an implicit understanding of natural law, where human society is compared unfavourably with more obedient nature (Isa. 1:3), and challenged for not fulfilling its role of sustaining the ordered structure of creation under God (Barton 2003). From passages such as Isaiah 24:3–6, it is clear that human wrongdoing was seen not simply to have an impact on humanity but to have caused the whole of creation to suffer undeservedly.

Isaiah paints a bleak picture of the present, but it is not a book that portrays a gloomy future. This is because its primary purpose was not to condemn but to encourage those prepared to examine their lives that there is hope for the future. This hope is conventionally understood from a human personal and social perspective, but the wonderful message of Isaiah is that salvation and redemption will be for the whole of creation as it finds its full, joyful and fruitful place in God's natural order of his redeemed universe (Isa. 65:17–25).

The latter part of the book, in particular, brings a message of expectancy. Isaiah 55:6–13, for example, does not describe a 'natural' ecosystem but a managed one, where God's care and sustaining of the earth is mirrored by careful human husbandry. It illustrates the effect of God's righteousness in terms of the natural fertility of the land and successful cultivation by those people who have returned to the Lord. This sustainable picture leads to the image of nature rejoicing in the Lord. The message of this passage (and indeed the overall message of Isaiah) is that as we turn to God in repentance and are redeemed by him, as we come under his rule and reign in the way we were always intended to do, so harmony will be mirrored in the rest of creation.

God of word and works

Chapter 55 forms the epilogue to the second part of Isaiah. At the start of the section printed at the beginning of this chapter, the twofold possibility that the wicked may repent and that God might give free pardon are seen as miracles difficult for humans to understand (Whybray 1981).

As we consider the emerging character of the twenty-first century, we are faced with significant problems. Some people justifiably fear that these will expand with terrifying ferocity as the century wears on, leading to despair that there can ever be a positive outcome to the processes we have set in train. Many have neither the faith to believe that the 'wicked will forsake their way', nor that God will really have mercy (Isa. 55:7). But that is not the biblical picture. For those prepared to take a long-term view, there are many texts in Scripture that provide us with a robust hope for the future. Just as there were many exiled in Babylon who never believed the people would return to Jerusalem and yet in time they did, so we can trust that God's purposes will continue to unfold. We should have courage that it is possible both for human hearts to change and for environmental processes to be moved in a life-giving direction.

Isaiah uses rain and the fertility of the earth as metaphors for the power of the word of God, and the transcendence of God's thinking compared to the rather more limited thoughts of humanity (Isa. 55:10–11). Since our Lord is the sustainer of all, his word is a means by which we can find the path towards sustainability, and his world is a daily miracle we can draw inspiration from. Despite all our worst efforts, nature does continue to be fruitful.

The promise of Isaiah 55 is that the fruitfulness we see now is only a glimpse of the potential fruitfulness that will one day be revealed.

A harmony with all creation

So how is this harmony portrayed? Looking at the images of nature in Isaiah, it is not a return to the hunter-gatherer existence of our ancient ancestors. We cannot go back to an idealized landscape of the past. Isaiah 45:18 can be translated to mean that God did not intend us to dwell in solitary places, but created the earth to be a 'safe dwelling' (Novak 2004). Though the wilderness is the place where we meet God and marvel at his creative power, it is not primarily where God places us in his work of restoration. Instead, we discover many examples of people finding true contentment in sustainably working and keeping the earth, fulfilling the commandments to us in the first two chapters of Genesis. Isaiah also describes how our farmed landscapes should relate to the more wild ones, by giving us a vision in which even wolves and lambs make peace with each other (Isa. 11:6–9; 65:17–25). There is harmony between farmed lands and wilderness: vineyards and mountains. It is possible to have both without one destroying the other.

One of the most pressing problems of our world is to balance human and environmental needs. We need to be able to farm and live, while enabling other species to survive and have the opportunity to flourish. The secret of this balance is to recognize that we are living on God's earth and it is he who sustains and providentially cares for it as the work of his hands. Once we have appreciated the intrinsic value of all creation we are better equipped to make the difficult decisions necessary to balance human and environmental concerns. We must do so with humility, however, remembering that only God can sustain the earth and that we need his mercy.

The call on those with faith in God is to declare the seriousness of our present situation to nations, organizations and individuals and to demonstrate the possibility of change in their own lives.

In previous generations, Christian reformers not only challenged injustice in society, but also became skilled in providing the needs for human reform: medical, educational, nutritional and social. These enabled people to have an increased quality of life and a personal life change, even if they did not embrace a Christian faith. The ethics that underlie the caring ideals of our society stem in part from the work of these reformers. Today, as we challenge society on environmental concerns, we need to equip ourselves with the skills needed for environmental reform so we can point to a practical pathway for change.

A harmony leading to new life

Isaiah 55:10 describes the earth bringing forth bread and wine. These ancient fruits of the soil are symbols of our new life in Christ. They embody our unity with one another as well as our communion with him. In the ancient Near East, sharing bread and wine was the traditional sign of reconciliation. Taking part in a fellowship meal entailed a commitment to cooperate and work together for the future. Jesus described himself as the bread of life, and the true vine. These images assume our involvement with the earth and our caring dominion of it. In other words, our relationship to the earth involves stewardship: farming the earth in a sustainable way will bring life to it; ignoring or neglecting our responsibility is likely to lead to its degradation or destruction. Using bread and wine to remind us of Christ's broken body and blood outpoured reminds us of the cost to Christ of our redemption, as well as the cost of restoring creation, that is groaning through the sin of humankind (Rom. 8:20–22).

In establishing bread and wine as a fellowship meal for the New Covenant, Jesus was echoing the vision of a restored creation where humans take a full part in caring for the earth and in doing so receive the blessing of its fruitfulness (Isa. 65:21; Luke 22:18). So in addition to their meaning of salvation for us, they are also symbols of restored sustainability, and a foretaste of the messianic banquet (Isa. 25:6–8).

Trusting God's faithfulness

The final image in Isaiah 55:12–13 is of creation rejoicing in the redemption of God's people. It speaks of a time in the future when humans will go forth in the peace of God and nature will joyfully receive those who could be described as its one-time oppressors. Briars and thorns are symbolic of fallen creation, and are replaced by those symbolic of fruitfulness. Non-sustainable agriculture frequently leads to land degradation and even desertification. All too often we have replaced trees and shrubs with tougher but less productive species that can survive on degraded soils. Pine trees and myrtles are symbols of a restored stability and fertility and provide hope for a reversal of this process and a regeneration of the soils and biodiversity. We not only have an optimistic picture of restoration but a promise that this fruitfulness will be an everlasting sign, which will not be destroyed.

A beautiful modern prayer is said at the end of the Communion service in the Anglican Church. It echoes the story of the prodigal son, who, on his return, was met by his father and received forgiveness and restoration. This prayer has an inspiring ending that has a particular relevance for the focus of this book:

> Keep us firm in the hope you have set before us,
> so we and all your children shall be free,
> and the whole earth live to praise your name;
> through Christ our Lord.
> Amen[1]

We can easily be overwhelmed by the size of the task we face in the call to rediscover our role as life-giving stewards for a sustainable earth, and our vocation to commend this path to the global community. In contrast, the message of Isaiah can seem too 'upbeat', and it is easy to lack faith in a positive future. But we

---

1. Prayer after communion, from *Common Worship*, © The Archbishop's Council, 2000.

cannot go back: our way must be to trust in the fruitfulness of the word of God and in his ultimate promises for his creation. Let us hope that when Christians break bread together and share the wine of the new covenant in Christ, we might hear more clearly a call to care for the earth that gives us bread and wine. Let us remember that Christ has chosen us to be fruitful with his word and bring his message of hope for the whole earth. As we go forth in faith, its ultimate redemption lies in his hands.

EPILOGUE: 'WE WILL HEAR YOU AGAIN ON THIS SUBJECT AT SOME OTHER TIME'

R. J. Berry

We cannot be all that God wants us to be without caring about the earth.

– Rick Warren

Those who heard Paul speak at a memorable meeting of the Areopagus in Athens were divided in their response (Acts 17:32–34). Some believed (and Paul doubtless rejoiced with them), some scoffed (there are those who will scoff at any novel or disturbing idea), while others were sufficiently interested to want to know more. Where, oh reader, do you stand, assuming you have read through the book and have not merely turned to the end to find the conclusion? The preceding chapters are written primarily to inform and convince, but inevitably also carry a challenge.

The danger is that this challenge will be lost in a mass of detail. It is pertinent to recall that Paul's address has also been criticized as lacking challenge on the grounds that it has no gospel content: Paul's recorded words mention neither Christ nor the cross (Acts 17:22–31).[1] John Stott slams this claim as gratuitous and unten-

---

1. Tom Wright (2005: 38) 'suspects' that the explanation for this criticism is 'the failure of past generations to come to terms with Paul's theology of

able. He points out (1990: 289) that Paul 'must have included Christ crucified. For how could he proclaim the resurrection without mentioning the death which preceded it?' Stott says further that

> The Areopagus address reveals the comprehensiveness of Paul's message. He proclaimed God in his fullness as Creator, Sustainer, Ruler, Father and Judge. He took in the whole of nature and of history. He passed the whole of time in review, from the creation to the consummation. He emphasized the greatness of God, not only as the beginning and the end of all things, but as the One to whom we owe our being and to whom we must give account . . . All this is part of the gospel. Or at least it is the indispensable background to the gospel, without which the gospel cannot effectively be preached . . . People are looking for an integrated world-view which makes sense of all their experience.
> (1990: 290)

The same response can be given to the text of this book. The various chapters touch on many of the components of the integrated world view John Stott recognized as needful; it is up to those who read them to assess and assemble them:

- *Climate change and its ramifying consequences*: now accepted by all but a few diehard refuseniks.
- *Biodiversity loss*: recognized and mourned, but its effects not fully appreciated.
- *Overconsumption*: generally condemned and rejected in theory but not much in practice.
- *Sustainable economics*: confusing to many because it involves complicated decisions and complex linkages, but convincing if all relevant factors are included ('internalized').

---

creation and covenant'. There is certainly a persistent unwillingness by evangelicals to explore the links between creation and covenant (Harris 2000). Wright himself documents the centrality for Paul of the links in a chapter 'Creation and Covenant' in his book *Paul: Fresh Perspectives* (Wright 2005).

- *Agriculture*: much disorderlessness, suffering from a perception of glut in some countries and compounded by drought and soil loss in others.
- *Water*: according to Joanne Green (Chapter 8), there is sufficient water for all, but it is crassly and unjustly mismanaged in many parts of the world (Clarke 2003).
- *Waste*: climbing up people's awareness, but not yet taken seriously.

Some environmentalists have been unhelpful in exaggerating the dangers of climate change or the effects of pollution. Their scare stories have been counterproductive. It is important for us to be rigorously honest in our assessments of environmental misuse. Recently, Stuart Pimm examined the major claims of the green alarmist lobby. He found that they were generally correct. For example, 'Human beings use 40 percent of annual terrestrial plant growth, 60 percent of accessible freshwater runoff, and 35 percent of the oceans' continental shelf productivity. These are large numbers, especially since our population will likely double by mid-century' (2001: 177). He concludes, 'The extent of our impacts is too obvious to miss, the consequences too serious to dismiss . . . There is much more that we need to know, but we clearly know enough to act. Our world is a spectacularly beautiful, interesting, and diverse place. Only by attending to its problems will it remain so' (248).

The secular 'world' will attend to environmental problems because of fear and self-interest. The tragedy is that Christians have a better and more coherent motive: creation care is a task laid on the church to proclaim and for believers to act. We should be in the lead: we have a moral responsibility, which is also an evangelistic opportunity. John Stott (1990: 290–291) ends his commentary on Acts 17 as follows:

> If we do not speak like Paul or feel like Paul, this is because we do not see like Paul. That was the order: he saw, he felt, he spoke. When Paul walked round Athens, he did not just 'notice' the idols. The Greek verb used three times (16, 22, 23) is either *theōreō* or *anatheōreō* and means to 'observe' or 'consider'. So he looked and looked, and thought and thought, until the fires of holy indignation were kindled within him.

May we be faithful and as objective as possible as we examine what we have done (and are doing) to creation, and then the fires of holy indignation may perhaps be kindled in us as we see what is being done to the world and to our children's heritage. Creation care is not an option for some: it is a task and privilege laid on all of us. Do we scoff? Or want to hear more? Or are we convinced?

> Praise the LORD from the earth,
>   you sea monsters and ocean depths;
> fire and hail, snow and ice,
>   gales of wind that obey his voice;
> all mountains and hills;
>   all fruit trees and cedars;
> wild animals and all cattle,
>   creeping things and winged birds.
> Let kings and all commoners,
>   princes and rulers over the whole earth,
> youths and girls,
>   old and young together,
> let them praise the name of the LORD,
>   For his name is high above all others,
> and his majesty above earth and heaven.
> (Psalm 148:7–13)

REFERENCES AND FURTHER READING

Arrow, J. K., P. Dasgupta, L. Goulder, G. Daly, P. R. Ehrlich, G. M. Heal, S. Levin, K.-G. Maler, S. Schneider, D. M. Starrett and B. Walker (2004). Are we consuming too much? *Journal of Economic Perspectives* 18: 147–172.

Arrow, K. (1974). *The Limits of Organization*. New York: Norton.

Arrow, K., A. Sen and K. Suzumura (eds.) (1997). The functions of social choice theory. In *Social Choice Re-Examined* 1: 3–9. London: Macmillan.

Barclay, O. R. (2006). Design in nature. *Science & Christian Belief* 18: 49–61.

Barton, J. (2003). *Understanding Old Testament Ethics: Approaches and Explorations*. Louisville, K Y: Westminster / John Knox Press.

Batchelor, P. G. (1993). *People in Rural Development*. Carlisle: Paternoster.

Bauckham, R. (2002). *God and the Crisis of Freedom*. Louisville, KY: John Knox Press.

Bauckham, R., and T. Hart (1999). *Hope against Hope: Christian Eschatology in Contemporary Context*. London: Darton, Longman & Todd.

Beisner, C. (1997). *Where Garden Meets Wilderness*. Grand Rapids, MI: Eerdmans.

Benedict XVI (2005). Inaugural address. *Boston Catholic Journal*, 24 April (http://www.boston-catholic-journal.com/inaugural_address_of_Pope_Benedict_XVI.htm).

Berry, R. J. (1972). *Ecology and Ethics*. London: IVP.

—— (1999). A worldwide ethic for sustainable living. *Ethics, Place and Environment* 2: 97–107.

—— (2003). *God's Book of Works*. London: T. & T. Clark.

—— (ed.) (2006). *Environmental Stewardship*. London: T. & T. Clark.

—— (in the press). Eden and ecology; evolution and eschatology. *Science & Christian Belief* 18.

Bimson, J. J. (2006). Reconsidering a cosmic fall. *Science & Christian Belief* 18: 63–81.

Birnie, P. W., and A. Boyle (1995). *Basic Documents on International Law and the Environment.* Oxford: Clarendon Press.

Black, J. (1970). *The Dominion of Man.* Edinburgh: Edinburgh University Press.

Blair, T. (1999). Foreword. *in A Better Quality of Life.* Cm 3545. Norwich: Stationery Office.

Blocher, H. (1984). *In the Beginning.* Leicester: IVP.

Boff, L. (2003). Unsustainable development. *National Catholic Reporter* 1.5, 30 April.

Boulding, K. (1966). The economics of the coming Spaceship Earth. In *Environmental Quality in a Growing Economy,* 77–82. H. Jarrett (ed.). Baltimore: Johns Hopkins Press.

Bouma-Prediger, S. (2001). *For the Beauty of the Earth.* Grand Rapids, MI: Baker Academic.

Bouma-Prediger, S., and P. Bakken (eds.) (2000). *Evocations of Grace: The Writings of Joseph Sittler on Ecology, Theology and Ethics.* Grand Rapids, MI: Eerdmans.

Boyer, P. (1992). *When Time Shall Be No More.* Cambridge, MA: Harvard University Press.

Brandt, D. (ed.) (2002). *God's Stewards.* Monrovia, CA: World Vision.

Bratton, S. P. (1983). The ecotheology of James Watt. *Environmental Ethics* 5: 225–236.

Brenton, D. (1994). *The Greening of Machiavelli.* London: Earthscan.

Bruce, D., and A. Bruce (eds.) (1998). *Engineering Genesis: The Ethics of Genetic Engineering in Non-human Species.* London: Earthscan.

Bruce, D., and D. Horrocks (eds.) (2001). *Modifying Creation? GM Crops and Foods: A Christian Perspective.* Carlisle: Paternoster Press.

Brueggemann, W. (2002). *The Land,* 2nd ed. Minneapolis, MN: Fortress Press.

Brunk, C. G. (2006). Public knowledge, public trust: understanding the 'knowledge deficit'. *Community Genetics* 9: 178–183.

Bryant, J. A., L. Baggott la Velle and J. Searle (2005). *Introduction to Bioethics.* Chichester: Wiley.

Bryant, J. A., and J. Searle (2004). *Life in our Hands.* Leicester: IVP.

Bryson, B. (2004). *A Short History of Nearly Everything.* London: Black Swan.

Buckminster Fuller, R. (1963). *Operating Manual for Spaceship Earth.* New York: Dutton.

Burke, E. J., S. J. Brown and N. Christidis (2006). Modelling the recent evolution of global drought and projections for the 21st century with the

Hadley Centre climate model. *Journal of Hydrometeorology*: 1113–1125.

Burnham T., and J. Phelan (2000). *Mean Genes: from Sex to Money to Food – Taming Our Primal Instincts*. Cambridge, MA: Perseus.

Calvin, J. (1847). *Genesis*, trans. J. King. Edinburgh: Banner of Truth Trust.

Cairncross, F. (2006). We must start adapting to climate change. *Independent*, 5 September 2006 (http://comment.independent.co.uk/commentators/article1362663.ece).

Carew-Reid, J., R. Presott-Allen, S. Bass and B. Dalal-Clayton (1994). *Strategies for National Sustainable Development*. London: Earthscan.

Caring for the Earth (1991). Gland, Switzerland: IUCN.

Carson, R. (1962). *Silent Spring*. Boston, MA: Houghton Mifflin.

Centre for Science and Environment (1999). *Citizens Fifth Report*. Delhi: Centre for Science and Environment.

Churches Together in Britain and Ireland (2005). *Prosperity with a Purpose: Christians and the Ethics of Affluence*. London: Churches Together in Britain and Ireland.

Clarke, T. (2003). The world's forgotten crisis. *Nature* 422: 251–256.

Clayton, P. (2004). *Mind and Emergence: From Quantum to Consciousness*. Oxford: Oxford University Press.

Clover, C. (2004). *The End of the Line: How Overfishing Is Changing the World and What We Eat*. London: Ebury.

Coase, R. H. (1960). The problem of social cost. *Journal of Law and Economics* 3: 1–44.

Cobb, J. B. (1972). *Is It Too Late?* Beverley Hills, CA: Bruce.

Costa, F. J., and A. G. Noble (1999). Conservation and the emergence of the sustainability concept. In *Preserving the Legacy: Concepts in Support of Sustainability*, 3–17. A. G. Noble and F. J. Costa (eds.). Lanham, MD: Lexington Books.

Costanza, R. (2006). Enough is enough. *Nature* 439: 789.

Costanza, R., R. d'Arge, R. de Groot, S. Farber, M. Grasso, B. Hannon, K. Limburg, S. Naeem, R. V. O'Neill, J. Paruelo, R. G. Raskin, P. Sutton and M. van den Belt (1997). The value of the world's ecosystem services and natural capital. *Nature* 387: 254–260.

Coward, H. (ed.) (1995). *Population, Consumption, and the Environment: Religious and Secular Responses*. Albany, NY: State University of New York Press.

Curry, D. T. Y., H. Browning, P. Davis, I. Ferguson, D. Hutton, J. DeAnne, F. Reynolds, M. Tinsley, D. Varney and G. Wynne (2002). *Farming and Food: A Sustainable Future*. London: DEFRA.

Daly, H., and J. Cobb (1989). *For the Common Good: Redirecting the Economy toward Community, the Environment, and a Sustainable Future.* Boston: Beacon Press. Danish Committees on Scientific Dishonesty (2003). (Original reports in Danish; English summary available at http://forsk.dk/portal/page/pro4/.)

Darwin, C. R. (1859). *The Origin of Species.* London: John Murray.

Dasgupta, P. (1998). The economics of food. In *Feeding a World Population of More Than Eight Billion People*, 19–36. J. C. Waterlow, D. G. Armstrong, L. Fowden and R. Riley (eds.). New York: Oxford University Press.

—— (2001). *Human Well-Being and the Natural Environment.* Oxford: Oxford University Press.

Dawkins, R. (2001). Sustainability doesn't come naturally: an evolutionary perspective on values. *Values Platform for Sustainability.* Inaugural Lecture, Environment Foundation, Royal Institution.

DEFRA (2003). Changing patterns: the UK Government Framework for Sustainable Consumption and Production (www.defra.gov.uk/environment/business/scp).

De Pomerai, D. (2002). Human use of non-human animals: a biologist's view. In *Bioethics for Scientists*, 86–99. J. Bryant, L. Baggott la Velle and J. Searle (eds.). Chichester: Wiley.

DFID (2004). *Water Action Plan.* London: Department for International Development.

Diamond, J. (2005). *Collapse: How Societies Choose to Fall or Succeed.* New York: Viking.

Donovan, N., and D. Halpern (2002). *Life Satisfaction: The State of Knowledge and Implications for Government.* London: Cabinet Office.

Downham, S. (2005). Talk at New Wine Conference, 28 July. Tape NEWA01395, available from ICC Tapes.

Dubos, R. (1973). *A God Within.* London: Angus & Robertson.

Duckham, A. N., and G. B. Masefield (1970). *Farming Systems of the World.* London: Chatto & Windus.

Durning, A. T. (1992). *How Much Is Enough? The Consumer Society and the Future of the Earth.* Worldwatch Environmental Alert Series. New York: Norton.

Easterlin, R. A. (2000). *Income and Happiness: Towards a Unified Theory.* Los Angeles: University of Southern California.

Ecologist (1972). *A Blueprint for Survival*, January (also published by Penguin Books, 1972).

Economist (2004). Putting the world to rights, 5–11 June: 59–61.

Ehrlich, P. R. (1968). *The Population Bomb.* New York: Ballantine Books.

Environmental Sustainability Index (2005). Benchmarking National Environmental Stewardship (www.yale.edu/esi).

Fewtrell, L., R. B. Kaufmann, D. Kay, W. Enanoria, L. Haller and J. M. Colford (2005). Water, sanitation and hygiene interventions to reduce diarrhoea in Less Developed Countries: a systematic review and meta-analysis. *Lancet Infectious Diseases* 5: 42–52.

Finger, T. (1998). *Evangelicals, Eschatology and the Environment.* Wynnewood, PA: Evangelical Environmental Network.

FitzRoy, F., and I. Smith (2004). Welfare, growth and environment: a sceptical review of *The Skeptical Environmentalist* by B. Lomborg. *Scottish Journal of Political Economy* 51: 707–717.

Forrester, D. B. (2001). Social justice and welfare. In *Christian Ethics*, 195–208. R. Gill (ed.). Cambridge: Cambridge University Press.

Foxwood, N., and J. E. Green (2004). *Thirsty World: A Briefing and Policy Paper.* Teddington: Tearfund.

Francis of Assisi (1959). *Saint Francis of Assisi: His Life and Writings as Recorded by Contemporaries*, trans. L. Sherley-Price. London: Mowbray.

Frey, B. S., and A. Stutzer (2002). *Happiness and Economics.* Princeton: Princeton University Press.

Gallup (2005). *The Gallup Poll of China: A 10 Year Study of Change* (www.gallup.com/poll).

Gore, A. (2006). *An Inconvenient Truth.* New York: Rodale.

Gorringe, T. (2006). *Harvest: Food, Farming and the Churches.* London: SPCK.

Gorringe, T., and E. J. Wibberley (2002). Agriculture in rural and international economy: theological reflections and practical consequences. *Journal of the Royal Agricultural Society of England* 163: 149–156.

Gould, S. J. (1993). The Golden Rule – a proper scale for our environmental values. In *Eight Little Piggies*, 41–51. London: Jonathan Cape.

Granberg-Michaelson, W. (ed.) (1987). *Tending the Garden.* Grand Rapids, MI: Eerdmans.

Haines, A., R. S. Kovats, D. Campbell-Lendrum and C. Corvalan (2006). Climate change and human health: impacts, vulnerability and mitigation. *Lancet* 367: 2101–2109.

Hall, D. J. (1986). *Imaging God: Dominion as Stewardship.* Grand Rapids, MI: Eerdmans.

Hamilton, C. (2003a) *Growth Fetish.* Crows Nest, NSW: Allen & Unwin.

—— (2003b) *Downshifting in Britain: A Sea-Change in the Pursuit of Happiness.*

Discussion Paper Number 58. Canberra: Australia Institute.

Hansen, J., L. Nazarenko, R. Ruedy, M. Sato, J. Willis, A. Del Genio, D. Koch, A. Lacis, K. Lo, S. Menon, T. Novakov, J. Perlwitz, G. Russell, G. A. Schmidt and N. Tausnev (2005). Earth's energy imbalance: confirmation and implications. *Science* 308: 1431–1435.

Harris, P. (2000). A new look at old passages. In *The Care of Creation*, 132–139. R. J. Berry (ed.). Leicester: IVP.

—— (2005). The world wide church – a last hope for the conservation of biodiversity? *Kairos Journal* (www.kairosjournal.org).

Hartwick, J. M. (1977). Intergenerational equity and the investing of rents from exhaustible resources. *American Economic Review* 67: 972–974.

Haught, J. (2005). Darwin, design and the promise of nature. *Science & Christian Belief* 17: 5–20.

Hawken, P., A. B. Lovins and L. H. Lovins (2000). *Natural Capitalism: The Next Industrial Revolution*. London: Earthscan.

Hay, D. A. (1989). *Economics Today: A Christian Critique*. Leicester: Apollos.

Heal, G. (1998). *Valuing the Future: Economic Theory and Sustainability*. New York: Columbia University Press.

Heap, R. B. (2003). Towards sustainable consumption – visionary or illusory. In *Transition to Sustainability in the 21 st Century*, 83–90. F. S. Rowland and P. N. Tandon (eds.). Washington, DC: National Academies Press.

—— (2004). Man and the future environment. *European Review* 12: 273–292.

Heap, R. B., and J. Kent (2000). *Towards Sustainable Consumption: A European Perspective*. London: Royal Society.

Helm, D. R. (1998). Environmental policy: objectives, instruments and institutions. *Oxford Review of Economic Policy* 14(4): 1–19.

Hepper, F. N. (1992). *The Illustrated Encyclopaedia of Bible Plants*. Leicester: IVP.

Hertwich, E. G. (2005). Consumption and the re-bound effect: an industrial ecology perspective. *Journal of Industrial Ecology* 9:1–6.

HM Government (2005). *Securing the Future: Delivering UK Sustainable Development Strategy*. London: Stationery Office.

Holdgate, M. W. (1996). *From Care to Action*. London: Earthscan.

—— (2006). Conservation grows a human face. In *Environmental Stewardship*, 234–243. R. J. Berry (ed.). London: T. & T. Clark.

Hore-Lacy, I. (2006). *Responsible Dominion*. Vancouver, BC: Regent College.

Houghton, J. T. (2004). *Global Warming: The Complete Briefing*, 3rd ed. Cambridge: Cambridge University Press.

—— (2005). Global warming. *Reports and Progress in Physics* 68: 1343–1403.

Houghton, J., and C. Henderson (2006). Reason and light. *New Statesman, Energy Supplement*, 15 May 2006, pp xviii–xix.

Hutton, G., and L. Haller (2004). *Evaluation of the Non-Health Costs and Benefits of Water and Sanitation Improvements at Global Level.* Geneva: WHO.

Intergovernmental Panel on Climate Change (2001). *Climate Change 2001*, 4 vols. Cambridge: Cambridge University Press.

IUCN (2006). *The IUCN Red List of Threatened Species.* Gland, Switzerland: IUCN.

Jackson, T. (2005). Live better by consuming less? Is there a 'double dividend' in sustainable consumption? *Journal of Industrial Ecology* 9: 51–68.

Jackson, T., and L. Michaelis (2003). *Policies for Sustainable Consumption.* London: Sustainable Development Commission Report.

Jacobs, P., and D. A. Munro (eds.) (1987). *Conservation with Equity: Strategies for Sustainable Development.* Gland, Switzerland: IUCN.

Jeeves, M. A., and R. J. Berry (1998). *Science, Life and Christian Belief.* Leicester: Apollos.

John Ray Initiative (1995). *A Christian Approach to the Environment.* Cheltenham: John Ray Initiative (originally published in *Transformation* 16: 72–113).

Jones, C. R. (1991). *Biblical Signposts for Agricultural Policy.* Leicester: ACF/UCCF.

Jones, J. (2003). *Jesus and the Earth.* London: SPCK.

Joy, D. C., and E. J. Wibberley (1979). *A Tropical Agriculture Handbook.* London: Cassell.

Jung, L. H. (2005). Healing and reconciliation as the basis for sustainability of life. *International Review of Mission* 94: 84–102.

Kasser, T. (2002). *The High Price of Materialism.* Cambridge, MA: MIT Press.

Kidner, D. (1967). *Genesis.* London: Tyndale.

King, D. (2005). Global warming: a clear and present danger. *Open Democracy*, 9 May 2005 (www.opendemocracy.net/debates).

King, F. H. (1911, repr. 1977). *Farmers of Forty Centuries.* New York: Rodale Press.

Küng, H. (1996). *Yes to a Global Ethic.* London: SCM Press.

Lawton, J. (in the press). Ecology, politics and policy. *Journal of Applied Ecology.*

Lawton, J., and R. M. May (eds.) (1995). *Extinction Rates.* Oxford: Oxford University Press.

Layard, R. (2005). *Happiness: Lessons from a New Science.* London: Allen Lane.

Leal, R. B. (2005). Negativity towards wilderness in the biblical record. *Ecotheology* 10: 364–381.

Leopold, A. (1949). *A Sand County Almanac.* New York: Oxford University Press.

Lomborg, B. (2001). *The Skeptical Environmentalist.* Cambridge: Cambridge University Press.

Lovelock, J. E. (1995). The greening of science. In *Science for the Earth*, 39–63. T. Wakeford and M. Walters (eds.). Chichester: Wiley.

—— (2006). *The Revenge of Gaia: Why the Earth Is Fighting Back – and How We Can Still Save Humanity.* London: Allen Lane.

Lubchenco, J., A. M. Olson, L. B. Brubaker, S. R. Carpenter, M. M. Holland, S. P. Hubbell, S. A. Levin, J. A. Macmahon, P. A. Matson, J. M. Melillo, H. A. Mooney, C. H. Peterson, H. R. Pulliam, L. A. Real, P. J. Regal and P. G. Risser (1992). The Sustainable Biosphere Initiative: an ecological research agenda. *Ecology* 72: 371–412.

MA (2005). *Millennium Ecosystem Assessment.* Nairobi: United Nations Environment Programme (www.millenniumassessment.org).

MacKay, D. M. (1991). *Behind the Eye.* Oxford: Blackwell.

Malthus, T. R. (1798). *An Essay on the Principle of Population, as it Affects the Future Improvement of Society.* London: Johnson.

Man in his Living Environment (1969). London: Church House.

Mathys, H. P. (2004). Creation in the Old Testament: an overview. *Listening to Creation Groaning*, 36–60. L. Vischer (ed.). Geneva: John Knox International Reformed Center.

McDonough, W., and M. Braungart (2002). *Cradle to Cradle.* New York: North Point Press.

Meadows, D. H., D. L. Meadows and J. Randers (1992). *Beyond the Limits: Global Collapse or a Sustainable Future.* London: Earthscan.

Meadows, D. H., D. L. Meadows, J. Randers and W. W. Behrens (1972). *The Limits to Growth.* New York: Universe Books.

Montefiore, H. (1969). *The Question Mark: The End of Homo Sapiens.* London: Collins.

Moore, A. (1889). The Christian doctrine of God. In *Lux Mundi*, 57–109. C. Gore (ed.). London: John Murray.

Mortimore, M. (2005). Dryland development: success stories from West Africa. *Environment* 47: 8–21.

Moule, C. F. D. (1964). *Man and Nature in the New Testament.* London: Athlone Press.

Murray, R. (1992). *The Cosmic Covenant: Biblical Themes of Justice, Peace and the Integrity of Creation*. London: Sheed & Ward.

Myers, D. G. (1992). *The Pursuit of Happiness*. New York: Avon Books.

—— (2002). *Social Psychology*. New York: McGraw-Hill.

Myers, N., and J. Kent (1995). *Environmental Exodus: An Emergent Crisis in the Global Arena*. Washington, DC: Climate Institute.

—— (2004). *The New Consumers*. Washington, DC: Island Press.

National Research Council (1999). *Our Common Journey: A Transition toward Sustainability*. Washington: National Academy Press.

Nature Conservancy Council (1984). *Nature Conservation in Great Britain*. Shrewsbury: NCC.

Nettle, D. (2005). *Happiness: The Science behind your Smile*. Oxford: Oxford University Press.

Newel, R., and W. Pizer (2000). *Discounting the Distant Future: How Much Do Uncertain Rates Increase Valuations?* Washington, DC: Resources for the Future.

Ng, Y.-K. (1997). A case for happiness, cardinalism, and interpersonal comparability. *Economic Journal* 107: 1848–1858.

Noble, A. G., and F. J. Costa (eds.) (1999). *Preserving the Legacy: Concepts in Support of Sustainability*. Lanham, MD: Lexington Books.

Northcott, M. S. (1996). *The Environment and Christian Ethics*. Cambridge: Cambridge University Press.

—— (2001). Ecology and Christian ethics. In *Christian Ethics*, 209–227. R. Gill (ed.). Cambridge: Cambridge University Press.

—— (2004). *An Angel Directs the Storm*. London: I. B. Taurus.

Novak, D. (2004). Is natural law a border concept between Judaism and Christianity? *Journal of Religious Ethics* 32: 237–254.

O'Donovan, O. M. T. (1986). *Resurrection and Moral Order*. Leicester: IVP.

Oeschlaeger, M. (1994). *Caring for Creation: An Ecumenical Approach to the Environmental Crisis*. New Haven, CN: Yale University Press.

Oldreive, B. (1993). *Conservation Farming for Communal, Small-Scale, Resettlement and Co-operation Farmers of Zimbabwe*. London: Rio Tinto Foundation.

O'Rourke, D. (2005). Market movements: nongovernmental organization strategies to influence global production and consumption. *Journal of Industrial Ecology* 9: 115–128.

Pacala, S., and R. Socolow (2004). Stabilization wedges: solving the climate problem for the next 50 years with current technologies. *Science* 305: 968–972.

Palmer, C. (1992). Stewardship: a case study in environmental ethics. In *The Earth Beneath*, 67–86. I. Ball, M. Goodall, C. Palmer and J. Reader (eds.). London: SPCK.

Palmer, M., E. Bernhardt, E. Chornesky, S. Collins, A. Dobson, C. Duke, B. Gold, R. Jacobson, S. Kingsland, R. Kranz, M. Mappin, M. L. Martinez, F. Michell, J. Morse, M. Pace, M. Pascual, S. Palumbi, O. J. Reichman, A. Simons, A. Townsend and M. Turner (2004). Ecology for a crowded planet. *Science* 304: 1251–1252

Palmer, T. N., and J. Raisanen (2002). Quantifying the risk of extreme seasonal precipitation events in a changing climate. *Nature* 415: 512–514.

Pezzey, J. V. C., and M. A. Tomin (2002). Progress and problems in the economics of sustainability. In *International Year Book of Environmental and Resource Economics: A Survey of Current Issues*, 165–232. T. Tietenberg and H. Folmer (eds.). Cheltenham: Edward Elgar.

Pimentel, D., C. Harvey, P. Resosudarmo, K. Sinclair, D. Kurz, M. McNair, S. Crist, L. Shpritz, L. Fitton, R. Saffouri and R. Blair (1995). Environmental and economic costs of soil erosion and conservation benefits. *Science* 267: 1117–1123.

Pimm, S. L. (2001). *The World According to Pimm*. New York: McGraw-Hill.

Pimm, S. L., and J. Harvey (2001). No need to worry about the future. *Nature* 414: 149–150.

Porritt, J. (2005). *Capitalism as if the World Matters*. London: Earthscan.

Porritt, S. (2006). Foreword. In *Sustainable Development and UK Faith Groups: Two Sides of the Same Coin?* 4–5. London: Sustainable Development Commission Report.

Postel, S. (1999). *Pillar of Sand: Can the Irrigation Miracle Last?* New York: Norton.

Potter, V. R. (1971). *Bioethics – Bridge to the Future*. Englewood Cliffs, NJ: Prentice Hall.

Prance, G. T. (1998). Indigenous non-timber benefits from tropical rainforest. In *Tropical Rainforest: A Wider Perspective*, 21–42. F. B. Goldsmith (ed.). London: Chapman & Hall.

Prance, G. T., and T. E. Elias (eds.) (1976). *Extinction Is Forever*. New York: New York Botanical Garden.

Pretty, J. (2002). *Agri-Culture: Re-Connecting People, Land and Nature*. London: Earthscan.

Quality of Life Counts (1999). *Indicators of Sustainable Development*. London: Stationery Office.

Rand, S. (2000). Love your neighbour as yourself. In *The Care of Creation*, 140–146. R. J. Berry (ed.). Leicester: IVP.

Rawls, J. (1971). *A Theory of Justice*. Cambridge, MA: Harvard University Press.

Reiss, M. J. (2002). Introduction to ethics and bioethics. In *Bioethics for Scientists*, 3–17. J. Bryant, L. Baggott la Velle and J. Searle (eds.). Chichester: Wiley.

Richardson, C. J., P. Reiss, N. A. Hussain, A. J. Alwash and D. J. Pool (2005). The restoration potential of the Mesopotamian marshes of Iraq. *Science* 307: 1307–1311.

Roach, R. (2005). *Dried up, Drowned out: Voices from the Developing World on a Changing Climate*. Teddington: Tearfund.

Rolston, H. (2002). Justifying sustainable development: a continuing ethical search. *Global Dialogue* 4: 104–113.

Ros-Tonen, M., W. Dijkman and E. L. van Bueren (1995). *Commercial and Sustainable Extraction of Non-Timber Forest Products*. Wageningen: Tropenbos Foundation.

Rowland, F. S., and M. J. Molina (1994) Ozone depletion 20 years after the alarm. *Chemical and Engineering News* 72: 8–13.

Santmire, P. (2003). Partnership with nature according to the scriptures: beyond the theology of stewardship. *Christian Scholar's Review* 32: 381–412.

Schaeffer, F. A. (1968). *Escape from Reason*. London: IVP.

—— (1970). *Pollution and the Death of Man*. London: Hodder & Stoughton.

—— (1973). *Back to Freedom and Dignity*. London: Hodder & Stoughton.

Schoch, R. (2006). *The Secrets of Happiness*. London: Profile Books.

Scientific American (2002). Misleading math about the Earth. January issue.

Securing the Future (2005). The UK Government Sustainable Development Strategy, Cm 6467. Norwich: Stationery Office.

Seligman, M. E. P. (2002). *Authentic Happiness: Using the New Positive Psychology to Realize Your Potential for Lasting Fulfilment*. New York: Free Press.

Sen, A. (2003). The ends and means of sustainability. In *Transition to Sustainability in the 21st Century*, 2–16. F. S. Rowland and P. N. Tandon (eds.). Washington, DC: National Academies Press.

—— (2004). Why we should preserve the spotted owl. In *London Review of Books*, 5 February.

Sheldon, J. K. (1989). Twenty-one years after the 'Historical roots of our ecologic crisis': how has the church responded? *Perspectives on Science and the Christian Faith* 41: 152–158.

Shellenberger, M., and T. Nordhaus (2004). *The Death of Environmentalism:*

Global Warming Politics in a Post-Environmental World (www.thebreak-through.org).

Sherley-Price, L. (1959). *Saint Francis of Assisi: His Life and Writings as Recorded by his Contemporaries.* London: Mowbray.

Shiva, V. (2000). *Stolen Harvest: Hijacking the Global Food Supply.* Cambridge, MA: South End Press.

Sizer, S. (2004). *Christian Zionism.* Leicester: IVP.

Sleeth, M. (2006). *Serve God, Save the Planet.* White River Junction, VT: Chelsea Green Publishing.

Smil, V. (1999). *Energies.* London: MIT Press.

—— (2001). *Enriching the Earth.* London: MIT Press.

—— (2003). *Energy at the Crossroads.* London: MIT Press.

Southgate, C. C. B. (2002). Introduction to environmental ethics. In *Bioethics for Scientists*, 39–55. J. Bryant, L. Baggott la Velle and J. Searle (eds.). Chichester: Wiley.

Spencer, R. W., D. K. Driessen and E. C. Beisner (2005). *An Examination of the Scientific, Ethical and Theological Implications of Climate Change Policy.* Burke, VT: Interfaith Stewardship Alliance/Acton Institute.

Spicer, J. (2006). *Biodiversity: A Beginner's Guide.* Oxford: Oneworld.

Stafford, D. A. (1983). Methane from farm wastes and energy recovery. In *Fuel Gas Developments*, 1–18. D. L. Wise (ed.). Oxford: CRC Press.

Stafford, D. A., R. R. West and A. D. White (1993). Review of occupational and environmental exposures to organics and associations with leukaemia and preleukaemia. In *Volatile Organic Compounds in the Environment*, 455–465. G. Leslie and R. Perry (eds.). London: IAI.

Stanhope, J., and G. Crawford (2006). Sins of the rich. *Tear Times*, autumn, 19–21.

Stern, N. (2006). *The Stern Review on the Economics of Climate Change.* Cambridge: Cambridge University Press.

Stott, J. R. W. (1972). *Understanding the Bible.* London: Scripture Union.

—— (1977). Obeying Christ in a changing world. In *Obeying Christ in a Changing World*, 9–31. J. R. W. Stott (ed.). London: Collins.

—— (1990). *The Message of Acts.* Leicester: IVP.

—— (2000). Foreword. In *The Care of Creation*, 7–9. R. J. Berry (ed.). Leicester: IVP.

Sustainable Development Commission (2004). *Redefining Prosperity: Resource Productivity, Economic Growth and Sustainable Development.* London: SDC Report.

—— (2004). *Shows Promise, but Must Try Harder.* London: SDC Report.

Takase, K., Y. Kondo and A. Washizu (2005). An analysis of sustainable consumption by the waste input-output model. *Journal of Industrial Ecology* 9: 201–220.

Taylor, J. V. (1975). *Enough Is Enough.* London: SCM.

Tearfund (2006a). *Pipe Dreams.* Teddington: Tearfund.

—— (2006b). *For Tomorrow Too.* Teddington: Tearfund.

This Common Inheritance (1990). White Paper on the Environment. Cm 1200. London: HMSO.

Tidball, D. (1999). *The Reality of Christ.* Fearn: Christian Focus Publications.

Tillett, S. (ed.) (2005). *Caring for Creation.* Oxford: Bible Reading Fellowship.

Tudge, C. (2004). *So Shall we Reap: What's Wrong with the World's Food and how to Fix it.* Harmondsworth: Penguin.

UN Department of Economic and Social Affairs (2004) Johannesburg Plan of Implementation (http://www.un.org/esa/sustdev/documents/WSSD_POI_PD/English/POIChapter4.htm).

UNESCO (2006). *Water: A Shared Responsibility. United Nations World Water Development Report 2.* Paris: UNESCO.

UNICEF (n.d.a) www.unicef.org/wes/index.

—— (n.d.b) www.unicef/infobycountry/nigeria.

United Nations Development Programme (2003). *Human Development Report, 2003.* New York: UNDP.

United Nations Environmental Programme (2002). *Global Environmental Outlook.* London: Earthscan.

—— (1995). *Global Biodiversity Assessment.* Cambridge: Cambridge University Press.

UN/WWAP (2003). *World Water Assessment Programme.* New York: United Nations.

Valerio, R. (2004). *L Is for Lifestyle.* Leicester: IVP.

Van der Zee, B. (2006). Campaign of the week: rail freight. *Guardian,* 5 September.

Von Weizsäcker, E., A. B. Lovins and L. H. Lovins (1997). *Factor Four: Doubling Wealth, Halving Resource Use.* London: Earthscan.

Ward, B., and R. Dubos (1972). *Only One Earth: The Care and Maintenance of a Small Planet.* London: André Deutsch.

WaterAid (2005). *Dying for the Toilet.* London: WaterAid.

WCS (1980). *World Conservation Strategy.* Gland, Switzerland: IUCN, WWF, UNEP.

Weitzman, M. (1998). Why the far distant future should be discounted at its lowest possible rate. *Journal of Environmental Economics and Management* 36: 201–208.

West, R. R., D. A. Stafford, A. Farrow and A. Jacobs (1995). Occupational and environmental exposures and myelodysplasia: a case-control study. *Leukaemia Research* 19: 127–139.

White, L. (1967). The historical roots of our ecologic crisis. *Science* 155: 1203–1207.

Whitney, E. (1993). Lynn White, ecotheology and history. *Environmental Ethics* 15: 151–169.

WHO (2004). *Evaluation of the Costs and Benefits of Water and Sanitation at the Global Level*. Geneva: WHO.

WHO/UNICEF (2000). *Global Water Supply and Sanitation Assessment*. Geneva: WHO.

—— (2004). *Meeting the MDG Drinking Water and Sanitation Target: A Mid-Term Assessment*. Geneva: WHO.

Whybray, R. N. (1981). *Isaiah 40–66*. New Century Bible Commentary. Grand Rapids, MI: Eerdmans.

Wibberley, E. J. (1989). *Cereal Husbandry*. Ipswich: Farming Press; New York: Diamond Enterprises.

—— (2003a). Integration towards ethical agriculture: challenges, principles and practice in international perspective. In *Biblical Holism and Agriculture: Cultivating Our Roots*, 203–248. D. J. Evans, R. J. Vos and K. P. Wright (eds.). Pasadena, CA: Willliam Carey Library.

—— (2003b). Creation, agriculture and genetic modification. *The Bible in Transmission*, spring, 14–17.

—— (2005). Leadership values and sustainable trading management for food security, biodiversity and equity. In *Developing Entrepreneurship Abilities to Feed the World in a Sustainable Way*, vol. 1, 333–345. International Farm Management Association Fifteenth World Congress, Campinas, Brazil (August).

Wilkinson, L. (ed.) (1991). *Earthkeeping in the Nineties*. Grand Rapids, MI: Eerdmans.

Wirzba, N., and S. Kingsolver (2003). *The Essential Agrarian Reader: The Future of Culture, Community and the Land*. Lexington, KY: University Press of Kentucky.

World Commission on Environment and Development (1987). *Our Common Future*. New York: Oxford University Press.

Worster, D. (1993). *The Wealth of Nature*. New York: Oxford University Press.

Wright, C. J. H. (2004). *Old Testament Ethics for the People of God*. Leicester: IVP.

Wright, N. T. (1999a). *New Heavens, New Earth*. Cambridge: Grove Booklet B11.

—— (1999b). New exodus, new narrative: the narrative structure of Romans 3–8. In *Romans and the People of God*, 26–35. S. K. Soderlund and N. T. Wright (eds.). Grand Rapids, MI: Eerdmans.

—— (2003). *The Resurrection of the Son of God*. London: SPCK.

—— (2005). *Paul: Fresh Perspectives*. London: SPCK.

Wroe, M., and Doney, M. (2004). *The Rough Guide to a Better World and how you Can Make a Difference*. London: Rough Guides/DFID.

GENERAL INDEX

SCRIPTURE INDEX